Universal Health Coverage for Inclusive
and Sustainable Development

Universal Health Coverage for Inclusive and Sustainable Development

A Synthesis of 11 Country Case Studies

Akiko Maeda, Edson Araujo, Cheryl Cashin, Joseph Harris, Naoki Ikegami, and Michael R. Reich

THE WORLD BANK
Washington, D.C.

Contents

Boxes

Figures

Tables

Foreword

Following the publication of the 2010 World Health Report, *Health Systems Financing: The Path to Universal Coverage*, low- and middle-income countries have shown growing interest in and demand for a systematic assessment of global experiences with universal health coverage (UHC), and for technical advice and investment support in designing and implementing UHC policies and programs.

In 2011, Japan celebrated the 50th anniversary of its own achievement of UHC. On this occasion, the government of Japan and the World Bank Group conceived the idea of undertaking a multicountry study to respond to this growing demand by sharing rich and varied country experiences from countries at different stages of adopting and implementing strategies for UHC, including Japan itself. This led to the formation of a joint Japan–World Bank research team under The Japan–World Bank Partnership Program for Universal Health Coverage. The program was set up as a two-year multicountry study to help fill the gap in knowledge about the policy decisions and implementation processes that countries undertake when they adopt the UHC goals.

We would like to thank the governments of the 11 countries that took part in the study for their willingness to share their data and experiences. The countries are Bangladesh, Brazil, Ethiopia, France, Ghana, Indonesia, Japan, Peru, Thailand, Turkey, and Vietnam. These 11 represent countries with very diverse geographic, economic, and historical contexts. This report synthesizes the main findings from the 11 country case studies using a common framework for analysis focused on the political economy of UHC reform and the policies and strategies for addressing challenges in health financing and human resources for health.

We would also like to extend our appreciation to the government of Japan for providing financial resources to conduct these country studies. The initial findings from the 11 studies were presented at the Global Conference on Universal Health Coverage for Inclusive and Sustainable Growth, held in Tokyo on December 5–6, 2013. At the conference, Japan's Deputy Prime Minister Taro Aso and World Bank Group President Jim Yong Kim jointly made the case for UHC as one of the essential goals for countries to aspire to for inclusive and sustainable development.

The goals of UHC are to ensure that all people can access quality health services, to safeguard all people from public health risks, and to protect all people from impoverishment due to illness (whether from out-of-pocket payments or loss of income when a household member falls sick). Although the path to UHC is specific to each country, we believe that countries can benefit from the experiences of others in learning about different approaches and avoiding potential risks. It is our hope that the country cases described in this report will offer useful lessons that can be used by countries aspiring to adopt, achieve, and sustain UHC. Our aim is to share knowledge and contribute to building healthier, more equitable societies while improving their fiscal performance.

Keizo Takemi
Member of the House of Councilors
National Diet of Japan

Timothy Grant Evans
Senior Director for Health, Nutrition
  and Population
The World Bank Group

Acknowledgments

This study was supported through the PHRD Grant (Japan) as a joint partnership program between the government of Japan and the World Bank Group. The program was steered by the Program Coordination Committee, cochaired by Keizo Takemi, member of the House of Councilors of the National Diet of Japan, and Timothy Grant Evans, senior director for the Health, Nutrition and Population Network of the World Bank Group.

The preparation of this synthesis report was led by a team comprising Akiko Maeda, lead health specialist and task team leader for the World Bank Group, and co-team leaders Professor Naoki Ikegami, Department of Health Policy and Management, Keio University School of Medicine, and Professor Michael R. Reich, Taro Takemi Professor of International Health Policy, Harvard School of Public Health. The chapter on health financing was drafted with contributions from Cheryl Cashin, health economist for Results for Development; the chapter on political economy was drafted with contributions from Joseph Harris, assistant professor of sociology, Boston University; and the chapter on human resources for health was drafted with contributions from Edson Araujo, World Bank Group. Helene Barroy, Naoko Miake, Yusuke Tsugawa, and Irene Jillson provided substantial inputs to the overall structure of the report, ensuring consistency with the country studies, and organizing and preparing the data and figures. Jonathan Aspin edited the report, and Daniela Hoshino helped prepare the manuscript for publication.

The report's initial findings were presented at the Global Conference on Universal Health Coverage for Inclusive and Sustainable Growth held in Tokyo on December 5–6, 2013, and the report benefited from participant feedback. The report also benefited from peer review comments received from Jorge Coarasa, Michele Gragnolati, and Timothy Johnston (The World Bank Group); and Soonman Kwon (Seoul National University School of Public Health). Valuable comments were also received from James Buchan (University of Melbourne), Michael Borowitz (Global Fund to Fight AIDS, Tuberculosis and Malaria), and Joseph Kutzin (World Health Organization).

This report is a synthesis of the 11 country case studies on universal health coverage, namely Bangladesh, Brazil, Ethiopia, France, Ghana, Indonesia, Japan, Peru, Thailand, Turkey, and Vietnam. The report on Thailand was financed by that country's government, and the report on France was cofinanced with the Organisation for Economic Co-operation and Development (OECD).

The case study on Japan was itself made up of theme-based case studies analyzing in depth the country's experience with universal health coverage, including macroeconomic trends and political economy of reforms, health financing, health workforce issues, and public health. The organization and conduct of the Japan case studies were led by Professor Naoki Ikegami. These case studies are available in the companion book *Universal Health Coverage for Inclusive and Sustainable Development: Lessons from Japan* (Ikegami, forthcoming), and on the web.

The case studies from the other 10 countries are available in the series Universal Health Coverage for Inclusive and Sustainable Development: Country Summary Reports, which can be found at http://www.worldbank.org/en/topic /health/brief/uhc-japan. The authors are acknowledged below:

Bangladesh	Sameh El-Saharty and Helene Barroy, The World Bank Group; and Susan Powers, health economist/consultant
Brazil	Edson Araujo and Magnus Lindelow, The World Bank Group
Ethiopia	Huihui Wang and G. N. V. Ramana, The World Bank Group
France	Helene Barroy, The World Bank Group; Zeynap Or, Institut de recherche et de documentation en économie de la santé (IRDES); and Ankit Kumar, OECD
Ghana	Nathaniel Otoo, deputy chief, Ghana National Health Insurance Authority; Evelyn Awittor, Patricio Marquez, and Karima Saleh, The World Bank Group; and Cheryl Cashin, Results for Development
Indonesia	Puti Marzoeki, Ajay Tandon, Xiaolu Bi, and Eko Pambudi, The World Bank Group
Peru	Christel Vermeersch, Rory Narvaez, and Andre Medici, The World Bank Group
Thailand	Walaiporn Patcharanarumol, Viroj Tangcharoensathien, and Suwit Wibulpolprasert, International Health Policy Program, Thailand; and Peerapol Suthiwisesak, National Health Security Office, Thailand
Turkey	Ece Amber Ozcelik, The World Bank Group; and Meltem Aran, Development Analytics
Vietnam	Helene Barroy and Eva Jarawan, The World Bank Group; and Sarah Bales, health economist/consultant

About the Authors

Akiko Maeda is a lead health specialist at the World Bank's Health, Nutrition and Population Global Practice, with over 20 years of experience in the field of health and development economics. She has provided technical assistance and policy advice to governments in low- and middle-income countries in the areas of health finance and health services reforms, and she is currently leading the World Bank's global strategy on Human Resources for Health. Prior to joining the World Bank, she held various positions in UNDP, UNICEF, and the Asian Development Bank. She received a master of arts in biochemistry and molecular biology from Harvard University, and a PhD in health economics from Johns Hopkins School of Public Health.

Edson Araujo is an economist at the World Bank's Health, Nutrition and Population Global Practice. He works primarily on health workforce issues, and his current work includes the analysis of health labor markets, measurement of health workforce performance, and the application of stated preference methods to elicit health workers' employment preferences. Prior to joining the World Bank he worked as a health economist in the University College London (the United Kingdom), the Brazilian Ministry of Health, and the Federal University of Bahia (Brazil). He graduated in economics from the Federal University of Bahia and specialized in health economics at University of York (U.K.) and Queen Margaret University (U.K.).

Cheryl Cashin is a health economist specializing in the design, implementation, and evaluation of health financing policy. She is a senior fellow at Results for Development Institute and is leading the Provider Payment Initiative of the Joint Learning Network for Universal Health Coverage (JLN) under a grant from the Rockefeller Foundation. She continues to serve as a health financing consultant for the World Bank, World Health Organization, and other international technical partners. She is the lead author on the forthcoming book *Paying for Performance in Health Care: Implications for Health System Performance and Accountability* and is a coauthor of several World Bank publications, including *Designing and Implementing Health Care Provider Payment Systems: A How-To Manual*.

Joseph Harris is assistant professor of sociology at Boston University and served as specialist on the political economy of health care reform for the Japan–World Bank Partnership Program for Universal Health Coverage. His research explores the politics of universal coverage policy in Thailand, Brazil, and South Africa. Dr. Harris is past recipient of the Henry Luce Scholarship and a Fulbright-Hays Doctoral Dissertation Award. He holds a master's in public affairs from Princeton University's Woodrow Wilson School and a PhD in sociology from the University of Wisconsin-Madison. His work is forthcoming in the *Journal of Health Politics, Policy and Law* and has appeared in the *Journal of Contemporary Asia; Citizenship Studies;* and the *Journal of Peacebuilding and Development.*

Naoki Ikegami is professor and chair of the Department of Health Policy and Management at the School of Medicine, Keio University, from which he received his MD and PhD. He also received a master of arts degree in health services studies with distinction from Leeds University (the United Kingdom). During 1990–91, he was a visiting professor at the University of Pennsylvania's Wharton School and Medical School, and he has continued to be a senior fellow at Wharton. He is past president of the Japan Health Economics Association and the Japan Society of Healthcare Administration. His research areas are health policy, long-term care, and pharmacoeconomics.

Michael R. Reich is Taro Takemi Professor of International Health Policy at the Harvard School of Public Health. He received his PhD in political science from Yale University in 1981 and has been a member of the Harvard faculty since 1983. Dr. Reich has written widely about the political economy of health systems, health reform, and pharmaceutical policy. He is coauthor of *Getting Health Reform Right: A Guide to Improving Performance and Equity* (Oxford, 2004), and is coeditor-in-chief of a new peer-reviewed journal titled *Health Systems and Reform.*

Abbreviations

CBHI	community-based health insurance
GDP	gross domestic product
GP	general practitioner
HEP	Health Extension Program (Ethiopia)
HEWs	health extension workers (Ethiopia)
HRH	human resources for health
IRDES	Institut de recherche et de documentation en économie de la santé (France)
LMICs	low- and middle-income countries
NHIS	National Health Insurance Scheme (Ghana)
OECD	Organisation for Economic Co-operation and Development
PPP	purchasing power parity
SIS	Seguro Integral de Salud (Integrated Health Insurance, Peru)
SUS	Sistema Único de Saúde (Unified Health System, Brazil)
UCS	Universal Coverage Scheme (Thailand)
UHC	universal health coverage
UNICAT	Universal Health Coverage Assessment Tool
UNICO	Universal Health Coverage Challenge Program
WDI	World Development Indicators
WHO	World Health Organization

Overview

The goals of universal health coverage (UHC) are to ensure that all people can access quality health services, to safeguard all people from public health risks, and to protect all people from impoverishment due to illness, whether from out-of-pocket payments for health care or loss of income when a household member falls sick. Countries as diverse as Brazil, France, Japan, Thailand, and Turkey that have achieved UHC are showing how these programs can serve as vital mechanisms for improving the health and welfare of their citizens, and lay the foundation for economic growth and competitiveness grounded in the principles of equity and sustainability. Ensuring universal access to affordable, quality health services will be an important contribution to ending extreme poverty by 2030 and boosting shared prosperity in low-income and middle-income countries (LMICs), where most of the world's poor live.

Under the Japan–World Bank Partnership Program for UHC, 11 countries (shown in table O.1) from low-, middle-, and high-income groups were selected to represent a diversity of geographic and economic conditions. All these countries have committed to UHC as a key national aspiration, but are approaching it in different ways and are at different points in achieving or sustaining it.

Some countries aim to achieve UHC through national insurance systems that purchase services from public and private providers, while others such as Bangladesh, Brazil, and Ethiopia have worked toward providing better access to services through the public delivery system. Group 1 countries are still setting the national policy agenda for moving toward UHC; Group 2 countries have made substantial progress toward UHC but still face significant gaps in coverage; those in Group 3 have recently achieved many UHC policy goals but face new challenges in deepening and sustaining coverage; and Group 4 countries have mature health systems with UHC but are still having to adjust national policies to meet changing demographic and economic conditions.

Table O.1 The 11 Countries in the UHC Study

	Group 1	Group 2	Group 3	Group 4
Status of UHC policies and programs	Agenda setting; piloting new programs and developing new systems	Initial programs and systems in place, implementation in progress; need for further systems development and capacity building to address remaining uncovered population	Strong political leadership and citizen demand lead to new investments and UHC policy reforms; systems and programs develop to meet new demands	Mature systems and programs: adaptive systems enable continuous adjustments to meet changing demands
Status of health coverage	Low population coverage; at the early stage of UHC	Significant share of population gain access to services with financial protection, but population coverage is not yet universal and coverage gaps in access to services and financial protection remain	Universal population coverage achieved but countries are focusing on improving financial protection and quality of services	Universal coverage sustained with comprehensive access to health services and effective financial protection
Participating countries	Bangladesh Ethiopia	Ghana Indonesia Peru Vietnam	Brazil Thailand Turkey	France Japan

Note: UHC = universal health coverage.

Key Policy Messages

The 11 countries are committed to the goals of UHC, and are willing to explore and share their experiences with others. While each country's health system brings its own unique history and confronts its own set of challenges, each country's experiences offer valuable insights into some of the common challenges and opportunities faced by other countries at all stages of UHC. The following key policy messages emerge:

- Strong national and local political leadership and long-term commitment are required to achieve and sustain UHC. Adaptive and resilient leadership is required, capable of mobilizing and sustaining broad-based social support while managing a continuous process of political compromises among diverse interest groups without losing sight of the UHC goals.
- Countries need to invest in a robust and resilient primary care system to improve access as well as manage health care costs.
- Investments in public health programs to prevent public health risks and promote healthy living conditions are essential for effective and sustainable coverage.
- Economic growth helps with coverage expansion, but is not a sufficient condition for ensuring equitable coverage. Countries need to enact policies that redistribute resources and reduce disparities in access to affordable, quality care.
- Countries need to take a balanced approach between efforts to generate revenues and manage expenditures, while expanding coverage.

- Countries need a coordinated approach to scale up their health workforce to meet the growing demand for health services that accompany expansion of coverage. "Scaling up" goes beyond just adding new staff: It should take into account labor market conditions and workers' own career aspirations and working environment.

Framework for Analysis

A summary report on UHC for each country was prepared, based on a common analytical framework, which focused on three themes: (a) the political economy and policy process for adopting, achieving, and sustaining UHC; (b) health financing policies to enhance health coverage; and (c) human resources for health policies for achieving UHC. These themes were selected because political economy plays a key role in shaping policy decisions and yet has been a relatively neglected area of research, and because financing and human resources represent two critical elements in any health system but are often analyzed separately and their interactions are rarely systematically addressed.

Political Economy

The international development community has increasingly recognized that carefully crafted technical solutions may have little practical effect if political economy concerns are ignored. There is a growing recognition of the critical importance of political economy in enabling or constraining social and economic reforms. Because UHC reforms intentionally redistribute resources in the health sector and across households, these policies inevitably involve political trade-offs and negotiations. Therefore, understanding the political situation and negotiating with the various interest groups are essential components of moving toward UHC.

This study identified three UHC policy processes that confront distinct political economy challenges: (a) adopting UHC goals; (b) expanding health coverage; and (c) reducing inequities in coverage.

Adopting UHC Goals

The 11 country studies suggest that adoption of UHC as a national goal can occur in conjunction with a major social, economic, or political change. For example, UHC became a national priority following a period of financial crisis in Indonesia, Thailand, and Turkey; at the time of redemocratization in Brazil; and during post–World War II reconstruction efforts in France and Japan.

In these countries, moments of major upheaval created opportunities for breaking through interest-group resistance to reforms, and allowed innovative approaches to be adopted or advanced. These periods also generated broad-based social movements and opportunities for political leaders to mobilize support from diverse groups and create a sense of national solidarity to promote major reforms. For example, the adoption of UHC policies in Turkey benefited from strong executive leadership from the Minister of Health and the head of state, who worked to create broad popular support. In Brazil and Thailand, social movements played a catalytic role in putting UHC on the political agenda and in encouraging government leadership to adopt and implement those reforms.

The 11 country studies also suggest that economic growth was not a necessary condition for adoption of UHC policies, although growth was important in supporting the subsequent expansion of coverage. Brazil's commitment to UHC grew during a period of slow economic growth, pushed by the movement for democracy. Thailand also committed itself to its Universal Coverage Scheme in 2001, after the Asian financial crisis when macroeconomic growth prospects were still fragile. Countries in Group 1 (Bangladesh and Ethiopia) face significant macroeconomic constraints but have still adopted UHC as a policy goal as an expression of national aspirations and as a means to mobilize social and political support to undertake reform.

Expanding Health Coverage

While some countries have sought to cover their populations through a single program and others through a web of programs, all 11 countries used an incremental approach to UHC expansion. This step-by-step approach emerged from the complexity of expanding health coverage to all population groups: it takes time to develop the institutional and technical capacities to support and sustain efforts, and to garner political support from diverse interest groups.

In the course of expanding health coverage, many countries faced the need to review, revise, and at times undo previously decided policies and strategies. Countries making progress in expanding coverage do so by learning from past experiences and by taking corrective actions. This is especially evident in Group 2 countries, which have made good progress but face major challenges in sustaining that effort. For example, Ghana is celebrating its 10th anniversary of establishing the National Health Insurance Scheme, which integrated multiple community-based plans under a single national program, and has used the opportunity to reassess operations. The system has achieved 36 percent coverage of the population and now must tackle sustainability as a major concern, as expenditure per beneficiary has been outpacing revenues. In Vietnam, the Ministry of Health and Vietnam Social Security (the health purchaser) have undertaken a thorough assessment of the national health insurance system to propose consolidation adjustments in an upcoming revision of the Health Insurance Law. Peru has achieved major increases in health coverage, especially for the poor, and now needs to start addressing fragmentation in financing and service delivery. Indonesia is also moving toward consolidating multiple programs in a major effort to accelerate progress toward UHC.

Reducing Inequities in Coverage

Countries in this study that established social health insurance programs first provided insurance coverage to civil servants and formal sector workers, as these groups are politically influential, live in urban areas near existing health facilities, and have institutional relationships with government through paying taxes. Expanding coverage to poor and vulnerable populations often requires strong government commitment to overcome interest-group politics and ensure voice for the interests of marginalized groups. Group 3 countries are examples where social movements combined with political leadership to play a catalytic role in overcoming political obstacles. In Brazil and Thailand, social activists also became part of the government agencies responsible for implementing UHC and holding governments accountable for expanding coverage.

The country studies show that an incremental approach to expanding health coverage typically leads to the establishment of multiple risk pools for different population groups with different levels of coverage. Once set up, these multiple pools are politically difficult to integrate or harmonize, since any such measure would redistribute resources across organized interest groups. Group 2 countries are seeking to address this issue: Ghana has established a national health insurance program as a platform for creating a unified risk pool; Indonesia and Vietnam are also taking significant steps to integrate and harmonize the multiple risk pools to achieve greater equity in coverage.

Health Financing

Under health financing, this study reviewed national experiences in three areas: (a) raising revenues to expand and sustain coverage; (b) getting more value for money; and (c) managing effective pooling and redistribution of resources to ensure equity and financial protection.

Raising Revenues

All countries in the study faced challenges in finding the fiscal space to finance UHC policies and programs, since coverage expansion calls for a steep increase in public spending. Countries have found different approaches to securing the necessary budget funding to implement UHC. Priority in the government budget for health, alongside macroeconomic growth, has been important in enabling countries to expand population coverage and provide better financial protection. The study also found that governments do not often accompany their political commitment to UHC with an explicit financial pledge, such as earmarking revenue, and only three of the 11 countries (Brazil, France, and Ghana) have explicit earmarks. Other countries that have achieved UHC have done so without them, but have consistently kept their budgetary allocation to the health sector high on the political agenda.

Many countries are seeking to diversify sources of revenue for UHC, and strategies vary among countries at different stages on the road to UHC. France and Japan are seeking to reduce overreliance on payroll taxes (because these taxes no longer generate enough revenue because of aging populations) and are turning to other forms of tax revenues. Brazil has permitted the growth of private voluntary health insurance—initially introduced to supplement statutory coverage—but has gradually increased its share because of actual or perceived poor quality of services in the Unified Health System (Sistema Único de Saúde, or SUS). This move has increased the share of out-of-pocket spending and is eroding financial protection. Countries with a large informal sector such as Thailand have found it difficult to expand coverage through payroll taxes alone and have expanded their allocation to health through general revenues. By contrast, low-income countries such as Bangladesh and Ethiopia are seeking ways to expand their narrow tax base by introducing new payroll taxes under a social insurance program. But this approach has significant equity implications since it may risk steering government resources toward workers in the formal sector and away from less affluent farmers and informal sector workers.

Managing Expenditures Well and Ensuring Value for Money

All 11 countries are facing tight resource constraints in achieving or sustaining universal coverage. Managing expenditures is therefore critical at all stages of UHC. The study found that open-ended fee-for-service payment systems typically produce cost escalation, and that many countries introduce measures to contain costs. Those measures can, however, end up eroding coverage and undermining financial protection.

Countries that carefully manage the total resources in the system and strategically use efficiency levers have been more successful in managing costs without eroding coverage. In Thailand and Turkey, for example, effective policies included a balanced approach to prioritizing services and medicines for benefits package expansion, strong negotiation with pharmaceutical companies, and the leveraging of provider payment systems so as to bring more benefits to more people. In France, 20 years of health-budget deficits have started to decline in the past few years through measures including setting national spending targets, reforming provider payments for primary and acute care, and strengthening state stewardship on health insurance spending through rigorous monitoring.

Japan has a unique approach in its fee-for-service system, through its biennial revision of the fee schedule, which places strong downward pressure on total health spending, combined with a global cap. The country provides financial protection to households by restricting copayments for catastrophic health expenditures. These measures have helped the country mitigate and balance the coverage-eroding effects of its cost-control efforts. Other examples of expenditure management include encouraging utilization of more cost-effective services, such as emphasizing primary care in the benefits package and encouraging investment in facilities providing high-priority services.

Managing Risk Pooling and Redistribution of Resources

The study shows that providing universal coverage for the entire population requires different forms of cross-subsidization, from rich to poor and from low-risk groups (the young, for example) to high-risk populations (the elderly, for instance). The consolidation of insurance schemes has been used to improve cross-plan fairness in Group 3 countries as they move toward UHC: Turkey undertook major reforms to consolidate multiple insurance programs and achieve integration and cross-subsidization. Brazil's 1988 constitution consolidated multiple programs under the SUS, financed through general taxation. Thailand consolidated two major programs in 2001 under its Universal Coverage Scheme, which covers the largest number of beneficiaries and ensures cross-subsidization and equitable financial risk protection among beneficiaries within this group. However, Thailand still maintains three separate insurance programs, and per-beneficiary expenditure across the three is highly skewed because of the lack of redistribution *across* them.

Among Group 2 countries, Ghana has taken steps toward integrating multiple programs. Ghana has a single risk pool under its National Health Insurance Law, which redistributes resources from wealthy to poorer households through progressive general taxation for the majority of funding in the system and the redistributive function of the National Health Insurance Scheme. In Vietnam, efforts are being made to consolidate multiple funds, but the actual pooling of revenues and cross-subsidization of expenditures remain incomplete. Indonesia and Peru have recently passed legislation that will move the system toward better cooperation and/or harmonization between multiple programs.

In Group 4, Japan has maintained multiple risk pools, but through a combination of standardized benefits and provider payments across plans, intergovernmental transfers of subsidies, as well as transfers between funds, maintains equity in contributions and expenditures. However, these redistributive mechanisms are not keeping pace with the rapidly aging population, and there are widening disparities in premium rates collected by different risk pools and plans. Cross-subsidization and redistribution would be easier to achieve if Japan could create an integrated risk pool. But multiple programs are politically difficult to integrate or harmonize once established, largely because better-off entrenched groups do not want to see their premium rates increase.

Human Resources for Health

The development of well-trained and motivated health workers is an essential component of a national UHC strategy. All 11 countries have faced major challenges in the production, performance, and distribution of health workers for UHC.

Addressing the Health Worker Shortage

Countries that have committed to provide UHC need to develop strategies to increase the production of health workers to meet the growing and changing demand for health services. One core lesson of this study is that countries need to match their commitment to UHC with the capacity to deliver health services, which in turn depends critically on the availability of qualified and motivated health workers. The shortage of health workers is a global challenge, but is especially acute in countries in the early stages of UHC adoption and expansion (Groups 1 and 2). For these countries, meeting the workforce targets for UHC will require them to rethink traditional models of education and service delivery.

Universal Health Coverage for Inclusive and Sustainable Development
http://dx.doi.org/10.1596/978-1-4648-0297-3

Some countries have expanded the health workforce in a short time by broadening the recruitment pool and offering flexible career opportunities and nontraditional entry points to health workers. New categories of health workers can have shorter periods of education and can be developed and deployed faster. Examples include Brazil's community health workers and Ethiopia's health extension workers. These strategies can help build the workforce in underserved areas or in specialties, and so strengthen health services delivery. However, they also require changes in the way health care is delivered, a redefinition of the scope of practice and functions of different categories of health workers, and revisions to regulations on education and on standards of training and practice. These reforms may face resistance from professions, reflecting the importance of addressing the political economy dimensions of change.

Improving the Performance of Health Workers

Expanding the production of health workers needs to be accompanied by governance and regulatory reforms to ensure quality and appropriate skills of health workers. This issue has been especially important in Group 1 and 2 countries, which have seen a rapid proliferation of private and public education institutions without adequate quality regulation. These countries are focusing efforts on harmonizing and enhancing quality standards to produce health professionals.

But ensuring health worker availability is not enough in delivering effective health services: health workers need a safe and supportive work environment where they are motivated and enabled, as well as held accountable to perform according to expected standards of care. Countries are exploring different approaches to introducing incentives to improve health worker performance, including pay-for-performance measures that link financing more explicitly to performance. The country experiences suggest that while monetary incentives can be effective, they are not sufficient: nonmonetary incentives such as peer recognition and peer support are important factors that should be included in the design of incentive systems. The organization of the care delivery system to ensure that teams with an appropriate skills mix are in place, and the availability of essential supplies and equipment, are also critical factors enabling health workers to perform better.

Ensuring a More Equitable Distribution of Health Workers

All 11 countries are grappling with maldistribution of health workers. This issue is most challenging for countries in Groups 1 and 2, especially in recruiting and retaining health workers in rural and remote regions. Countries in Group 3 have made large improvements in reducing geographic disparities in distribution, and their experiences offer useful insights. Rural-urban disparities in distribution can be reduced through multiple strategies, including monetary and nonmonetary incentives, improvements in working conditions, supportive supervision in health facilities, and an education system that recruits graduates from these underserved communities (through scholarships and quotas for example), and prepares them for the working conditions found there. Compulsory service through bonding is another policy to encourage deployment in underserved areas.

Countries in Group 3 have used a combination of these policies to reduce geographic disparities, and many Group 2 countries are developing and implementing policies with a similar, multipronged approach. Experience from Group 3 countries also suggests that investing in primary health care workers and improving their working conditions have been essential in these countries' efforts to reduce coverage gaps because, while outlays in the hospital sector tend to skew the health workforce toward urban areas, investments in these workers tend to expand health service availability in underserved communities.

Conclusion

As countries commit to UHC and move toward that goal, they confront continuing challenges of making trade-offs and of balancing competing demands. Policy makers often face decisions that can be coverage enhancing or coverage eroding. Successful countries have made choices that are, on balance, coverage enhancing, and have learned from past challenges and have adapted their approaches. Learning from other countries, and adapting the lessons to local conditions, can help countries make progress toward UHC, adopt better policy decisions, and navigate real-world implementation challenges better.

Every country in the world can aspire to UHC, so as to improve the health and welfare of all their citizens and to help realize inclusive and sustainable development. It is not too early for low-income countries with little coverage to aim for UHC, as they can start building institutional capacity, learn from the experiences of other countries, and adapt innovative approaches emerging across the globe that can speed up coverage expansion. UHC priorities, strategies, and implementation plans will differ from one country to another, depending on local context. But the key policy messages listed earlier can help all countries develop and refine their own approaches to UHC, especially in making their policies accountable and transparent. The global community is committed to work together to support LMICs in their efforts to move toward UHC. The government of Japan and the World Bank Group stand ready to assist countries to achieve this goal.

CHAPTER 1

Goals of Universal Health Coverage

To end poverty and help to ensure shared prosperity, all countries need a sustainable, inclusive development strategy built on human capital investments in health, education, and social protection for all. To this end, there has been a growing movement across the globe for universal health coverage (UHC). UHC has been defined as a condition where all people who need health services (prevention, promotion, treatment, rehabilitation, and palliative care) receive them, without undue financial hardship (WHO 2010). UHC consists of three interrelated components: (a) the full spectrum of health services according to need; (b) financial protection from direct payment for health services when consumed; and (c) coverage for the entire population (figure 1.1).

There is no single approach to UHC. Some countries aim to achieve it through national insurance systems that purchase services from public and private providers, while others have worked toward providing better access to services through the public delivery system.

Opportunities: UHC Contributes to Inclusive and Sustainable Development

The World Bank Group aims to help countries build healthier, more equitable societies, as well as to improve their fiscal performance and country economic competitiveness—toward the goals of ending extreme poverty by 2030 and boosting shared prosperity. The World Bank Group is committed to UHC as a means of making sure that no family is forced into poverty because of health care expenses. Countries can tackle this injustice by introducing models of equitable health financing with strong social protection measures for all members of society. The World Bank Group will also endeavor to close the gap in access to quality health services for the poorest 40 percent of the population in every country. This requires a health system that ensures that health investments and expenditures contribute to improving health outcomes, equitably and sustainably.

Figure 1.1 Three Dimensions of UHC (the "UHC Cube")

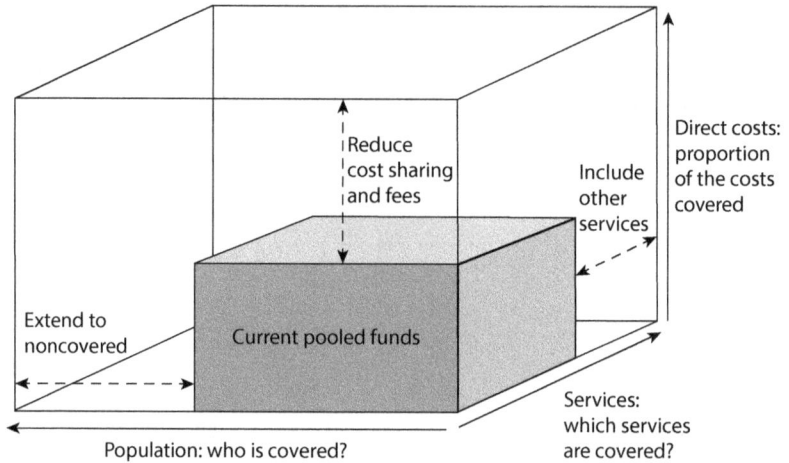

Source: WHO website, http://www.who.int/health_financing/strategy/dimensions/en.
Note: UHC = universal health coverage; WHO = World Health Organization.

To measure progress toward these goals, the World Bank Group has two overarching targets:

- For financial protection, by 2020, the proposed target is to reduce by half the number of people impoverished due to out-of-pocket health care expenses. By 2030, no one should fall into poverty because of such expenses. (The numbers: from 100 million people impoverished every year [Xu et al. 2007], to 50 million by 2020, and to zero by 2030.)
- For service delivery, the proposed target is to ensure that at least four out of every five of the people in the lowest income groups in every country have access to essential health services. This target covers the health-related Millennium Development Goals[1] and family planning, as well as the most prevalent chronic conditions and injuries.

Improving health outcomes is critical to building all individuals' capabilities and enabling them to compete for jobs that will let them share in the prosperity and opportunities generated for inclusive and sustainable development. Countries as diverse as Brazil, France, Japan, Thailand, and Turkey have achieved universal population coverage, and are showing how UHC programs can improve the health and welfare of their citizens, while laying the foundation for economic growth and competitiveness grounded in the principles of equity and sustainability.

Challenges: Adopt, Achieve, and Sustain

UHC offers a powerful aspiration for a country, but even after a government has adopted it as a goal, many obstacles to achieving and then sustaining it remain. Entrenched interest groups often stand in the way of reforms that threaten to overturn inequitable or ineffective arrangements. Health services themselves are highly susceptible to market failure, owing to difficulties in measuring and accounting for the use of resources and these resources' impact on quality, safety, and effectiveness. Another challenge is technological innovation, which is constantly changing service standards, raising questions about appropriate and equitable distribution, as well as requirements for safety, efficacy, and quality—just as demographic and epidemiological transitions are continuously transforming the nature of demand for health services.

Even in countries that have achieved UHC, still needed are the effective engagement of stakeholders, equitable distribution of resources and services, and able governance of programs. These requirements call for continuous monitoring and evaluation, including quality-improvement mechanisms, as well as regulation of health coverage and quality, all aimed to ensure that valuable public and private resources are used for priority goals and make significant and efficient contributions. They require commitment from all segments of society—elected officials, policy makers, health professionals, business leaders, and citizens themselves—to establish a robust governance structure that supports a resilient health system responsive to people's needs, and that can adapt to changing conditions.

The World Health Organization (WHO) and the World Bank Group are also jointly developing a common framework for UHC monitoring as part of a comprehensive framework for monitoring national health system performance (WHO and World Bank 2013). The framework will focus on two discrete components: coverage levels for health interventions and financial risk protection, both with a strong emphasis on equity.

The studies analyzed in this publication complement other major initiatives by the World Bank Group on UHC. The Universal Health Coverage Challenge Program (UNICO—see box 1.1) undertook 25 country case studies that focused on programs designed to extend health coverage to poor and vulnerable groups. UNICO will also develop a Universal Health Coverage Assessment Tool (UNICAT) to evaluate current country capacity to adopt UHC policies. These efforts, together, are part of a global effort to collect evidence and develop tools that can be used by countries moving toward UHC.

Box 1.1 Tools for UHC—UNICO and UNICAT

The World Bank promotes reduced extreme poverty and increased shared prosperity by supporting the efforts of countries to transition toward universal health coverage (UHC). The analogous objectives of UHC are to improve health outcomes, reduce the financial risks associated with ill-health, and increase equity across the population. The World Bank Group recognizes that there are many paths toward UHC and does not endorse any one or one set of organizational or financial arrangements. Regardless of path, the quality of the instruments

box continues next page

Box 1.1 Tools for UHC—UNICO and UNICAT *(continued)*

and institutions that countries establish (or reorient) to adopt and achieve UHC is essential to sustaining it.

The Universal Health Coverage Challenge Program (UNICO) consists of two efforts to develop and share operational toolboxes for moving toward UHC. The first involves the preparation of case studies that explore the "nuts and bolts" of programs in 25 countries, designed to expand health coverage from the bottom up (that is, starting with the poor and vulnerable). These studies have been published under the World Bank Group's Universal Health Coverage Study Series, and a synthesis comparing the 25 countries will be available in late 2014. The synthesis will assist countries to focus on equity, efficiency, and fiscal sustainability by using a framework that emphasizes three elements: the nuts and bolts of expanding the UHC cube; the supply and mode of health service delivery; and the use of monitoring to ensure accountability during implementation.

The second effort is in developing a Universal Health Coverage Assessment Tool (UNICAT) to help countries and partners assess the strengths and weaknesses of their capacity for executing UHC policies. The tool not only provides a factual capacity review, but also elicits opinions from a wide range of experts on the structural and political hurdles to achieving UHC in their country. The tool has been piloted in 15 countries and its results are being evaluated.

Note

1. Millennium Development Goals set targets to reduce childhood malnutrition, infant and child mortality rates, maternal mortality ratios, and mortality due to major communicable diseases (HIV/AIDS, malaria, and tuberculosis).

References

WHO (World Health Organization). 2010. *The World Health Report: Health Systems Financing: The Path to Universal Coverage.* Geneva. http://www.who.int/whr/en/index .html.

WHO and World Bank. 2013. "Monitoring Progress towards Universal Health Coverage at Country and Global Levels: A Framework." A discussion paper. http://www.who .int/healthinfo/country_monitoring_evaluation/UHC_WBG_DiscussionPaper _Dec2013.pdf.

Xu, K., D. B. Evans, G. Carrin, A. M. Aguilar-Rivera, P. Musgrove, and T. Evans. 2007. "Protecting Households from Catastrophic Health Spending." *Health Affairs* 26 (4): 972–83.

CHAPTER 2

Objectives, Scope, and Analytical Framework

Objectives and Scope

The Japan–World Bank Partnership Program study undertook in-depth country case studies to examine systematically the design and implementation of universal health coverage (UHC) policies and their outcomes, with the goal of describing how these policies were implemented and whether they led to expected results. Eleven countries at different stages of UHC were selected to take part.

The countries were deliberately chosen for diversity (table 2.1). They range from those at early stages of adoption to those with well-established UHC programs; are from several geographic regions; and have different health financing and delivery systems (such as social health insurance or a national health service). The countries also reflect different historical backgrounds (for example, the post–World War II era for France and Japan or the new millennium's reforms for Bangladesh). These countries were also selected for their commitment to UHC and their readiness to explore the key policy questions included in the analytical framework of the study (see "Framework for Analysis," which follows). The countries are placed into four broad groups, reflecting different stages of adopting, achieving, and sustaining UHC.

A case-study method was selected to focus on *how* each country uses different policy levers simultaneously for reaching UHC objectives. The outputs from these case studies are not intended to prescribe generalizable solutions, but rather to describe steps taken by countries that have enhanced (or eroded) UHC in order to identify good (or bad) practices as lessons to share with other countries. The findings from these studies are also intended to identify knowledge gaps for future research.

The program also included detailed studies of Japan's 50-year experience with UHC. They aim to identify potential lessons from Japan for low- and middle-income countries on policies that led to coverage-enhancing (alternatively, coverage-eroding) results. Highlights are in the companion volume

Table 2.1 Profile of Program Countries

Characteristics	Group 1	Group 2	Group 3	Group 4
Status of UHC policies and programs	Agenda setting; piloting new programs and developing new systems	Initial programs and systems in place, implementation in progress; need for further systems development and capacity building to address remaining uncovered population	Strong political leadership and citizen demand lead to new investments and UHC policy reforms; systems and programs develop to meet new demands	Mature systems and programs: adaptive systems enable continuous adjustments to meet changing demands
Status of health coverage	Low population coverage; at the early stage of UHC	Significant share of population gain access to services with financial protection, but population coverage is not yet universal and coverage gaps in access to services and financial protection remain	Universal population coverage achieved but countries are focusing on improving financial protection and quality of services	Universal coverage sustained with comprehensive access to health services and effective financial protection
Countries	Bangladesh Ethiopia	Ghana Indonesia Peru Vietnam	Brazil Thailand Turkey	France Japan

Note: UHC = universal health coverage.

Universal Health Coverage for Inclusive and Sustainable Development: Lessons from Japan (Ikegami, forthcoming).

Framework for Analysis

Given the multiplicity of actors and complexity of interactions that influence health coverage, it is daunting to identify key factors and different pathways that enhance or erode coverage (Kutzin 2012). For this reason, research on health systems and UHC has tended to disaggregate the system into its constituent parts and to examine isolated relationships in "silos" so that policy interventions and results can be more readily measured and evaluated. In reality, however, policy makers have to intervene in all aspects of the health system simultaneously and require a more holistic approach to address the difficult trade-offs and take advantage of potential synergies. For example, policies on health financing have a profound influence on, and in turn are influenced by, those related to health workforce availability, distribution, and performance. The interaction between these policy areas is one of the topics explored in this book.

A common framework for case-study analysis was used to examine policies and their impact on enhancing or eroding UHC. The case studies focused on three aspects of health systems: the political economy and its implications for the process of policy formulation, decision making, and implementation; the health financing system and associated policies; and the health service delivery system, with a focus on human resources (figure 2.1).

Figure 2.1 Aspects of the Health System Affecting Coverage

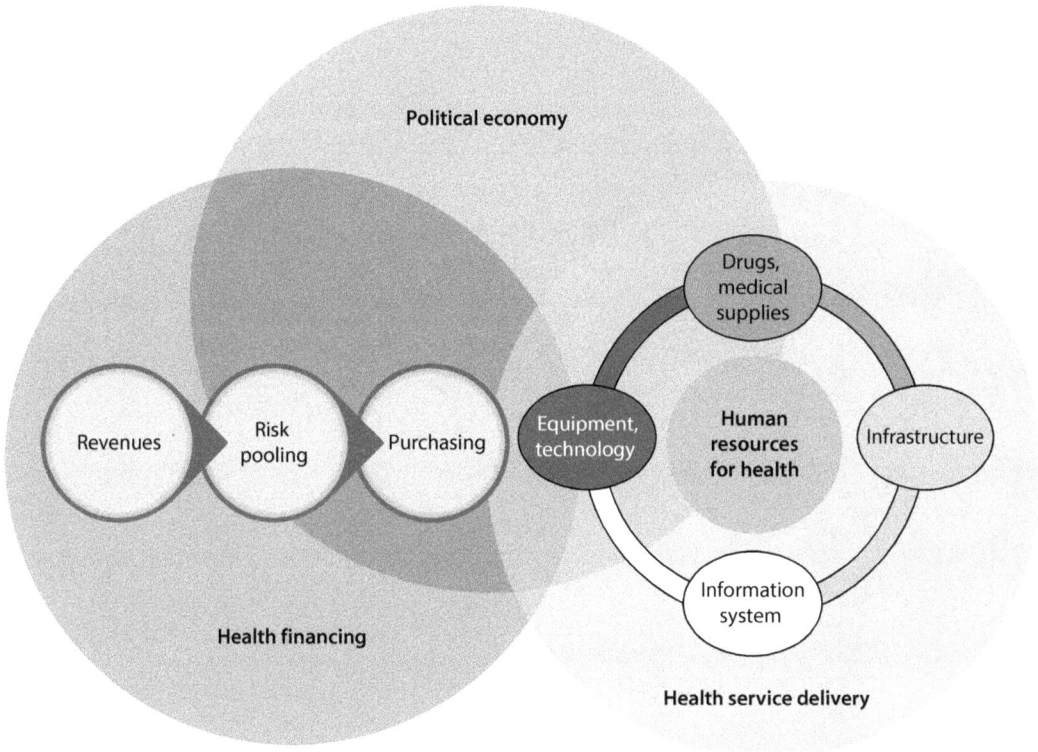

The health financing system covers the capacity to mobilize revenues, organize risk pools, and make payments for services. Health service delivery involves investments in a wide range of inputs, such as drugs, medical supplies, technology, and infrastructure, and most critically, the health workers who play a central role in delivering services and mediating all aspects of health care. The political economy and policy process context plays a major role in shaping policy decisions and how they are implemented. The case studies examine the interactions among these three aspects. They do not address many other important aspects such as demand-side policies and programs, or an in-depth analysis of impacts and importance of technology change, though this should not imply lower priority for these issues.

References

Ikegami, N., ed. Forthcoming. *Universal Health Coverage for Inclusive and Sustainable Development: Lessons from Japan.* Washington, DC: World Bank.

Kutzin, J. 2012. "Anything Goes on the Path to Universal Health Coverage? No." *Bulletin of the World Health Organization* 90: 867–68.

CHAPTER 3

Emerging Lessons from Country Experiences

As countries commit to adopting universal health coverage (UHC) and move along the stages toward achieving and sustaining it, they face a continuous challenge of trading off and balancing competing demands, and at any point their choices can either enhance or erode coverage. If political compromises or pressures of fiscal sustainability end in decisions that exclude coverage for some population groups, reduce benefits or access to services, or increase cost sharing, they erode coverage along one of the different dimensions of "coverage": population coverage, access to services, and financial protection. Policies that support strategic payment systems, or that lead to better-negotiated medicine prices and well-targeted subsidies, can enhance coverage, freeing resources to provide more people with better access to high-quality services with greater financial risk protection.

The line is sometimes blurred between policies that enhance or erode coverage. Some of the former when carried out too far can eventually put too much pressure on financial, human, and other resources and begin to erode coverage. For example, strategic cost sharing that directs patients to more cost-effective primary care services may eventually be coverage enhancing, but could also act as a barrier to access. Turkey's price negotiations with pharmaceutical companies and global spending caps have helped reduce the cost of medicines for UHC since 2008, thus helping free resources to expand coverage, but this approach is now showing signs of discouraging market participation and innovation among pharmaceutical companies by reducing their profits, which could eventually erode access to medicines.

Thus the stages toward UHC require a constant rebalancing that relies on regularly reassessing where the pressures on the system hurt and where new pressures can best be applied to maintain fiscal balance, to reallocate resources, and to align incentives to ensure equitable coverage. Ultimately, the countries that have been most successful in achieving and sustaining UHC have made choices at critical junctures that are, on balance, coverage enhancing;

have learned from their past mistakes; and have established a system that continuously absorbs lessons, and adapts.

The following section describes the experience of one of these countries—Japan—in achieving and sustaining UHC. It illustrates the complexity of reforms required, and the importance of continuous commitment and adjustment to sustain health coverage under changing socioeconomic conditions.

Special Country Feature—Japan's Experience in Achieving and Sustaining UHC[1]

Japan's political and historical context shows that the country made long-term commitments to UHC that persisted under different political conditions. Japan began its movement toward UHC before World War II as part of its preparation for war to develop a healthy workforce, and expansion continued during the war years. After the war, UHC was picked up by the governing political party as a national goal for social solidarity contributing to postwar recovery, and as a way to respond to challenges from opposition parties associated with socialist and communist movements.

Eventually compulsory arrangements were needed to expand coverage to the informal sector and other hard-to-reach groups, taking a variety of forms. Japan expanded health coverage to informal, self-employed, and unemployed populations through residence-based health insurance programs (Citizens Health Insurance) managed by municipalities. These plans were introduced on a voluntary basis for residents, and gradually expanded by increasing government subsidies to cover additional beneficiaries. They became mandatory for all residents once coverage exceeded 80 percent in that municipality, and those not covered by other health insurance plans were automatically enrolled in this program. Japan achieved UHC in 1961 when the last municipality reached mandatory enrollment status under its Citizens Health Insurance.

Economic growth can help provide fiscal space[2] for UHC. Japan's "Income-Doubling Plan" helped expand and sustain UHC. In the mid-1950s, nearly half the population was living near the poverty line, but in the 1960s the country enjoyed rapid economic growth, driven by the plan, designed by the economist Osamu Shimomura and introduced by Prime Minister Hayato Ikeda in 1960. The plan aimed to double real per capita national income in 10 years by achieving annual gross domestic product growth of 11 percent. In fact, income doubled by 1967, which helped to make it more affordable for Japanese citizens to pay the premiums to the social health insurance system, and for the government to allocate more funds to health.

Redistribution mechanisms and policies to harmonize benefits and payment systems have played a key role in reducing inequities across multiple insurance programs. Japan incrementally expanded health coverage through multiple health programs covering different categories of insured groups. Over time, it harmonized entitlements to the same benefits and had the same cost sharing for people of the same age group. However, the financial base to meet these standards varies across health insurance plans, because the age distribution and risk profiles of enrollees are highly imbalanced. To address these disparities, transfers are made from the central and local governments and other health insurance programs to the Citizens Health Insurance programs, and within them, greater amounts to programs that have high proportions of these enrollees. Although these redistribution mechanisms have improved equity across plans and population groups, the contributions as a share of income still vary across population groups. In recent years, changes in the employment and demographic profiles of beneficiaries have led to growing disparities in contribution rates across different groups, which the existing redistribution mechanism has been unable to address, highlighting the risk of creating multiple health plans that require complex redistribution systems to maintain equity.

Managing health spending under a single payment system has helped the government to maintain strong control over total health expenditure. Japan manages its health care expenditures through its single payment system and the fee schedule set by the government. This schedule is revised every two years, first by setting a global price revision rate, and then by revising the price and conditions of billing on all the services and drugs on an item-by-item basis. Adherence to these conditions is regularly audited, which has mitigated inappropriate utilization of services. The payment system also prohibits balance billing (charging fees to patients above the price set in the fee schedule) by providers and strictly restricts extra billing (charging services listed in the fee schedule with those that are not). These measures have helped Japan control health care expenditures: in 2011 total health spending was 9.6 percent of gross domestic product—just above the average for the Organisation for Economic Co-operation and Development—an impressive achievement, given that Japan has the oldest population in the world.

Japan's fee schedule has also been used to influence the behavior of health care providers. It not only sets prices, but also establishes an institutionalized process of negotiating resource allocation and benefits among key stakeholders, by setting conditions for reimbursements. For example, the fee schedule provides detailed conditions of payments, such as nurse staffing levels and diagnosis criteria for procedures. The biennial revision provides an important platform for reviewing and revising priorities, negotiating trade-offs, and involving all the stakeholders in a continuous process of adjustment to meet the health sector's strategic objectives and directions.

Japan has introduced multiple policies to ensure equitable access to and distribution of health services and health workers. Although 80 percent of hospitals and nearly all clinics are in the private sector, they are all integrated into the delivery system because more than 90 percent of their revenues are derived from services regulated by the fee schedule. Public sector hospitals have additional revenues in the form of subsidies from national and local government general budgets. In 2004, Japan introduced major reforms in the organization of its national government-run hospitals to improve efficiency. Although the fee schedule system places considerable pressures on health care providers to run their services efficiently, these hospitals had been insulated by the high subsidies from the government budget. Under the 2004 reform, Japan created a single independent nonprofit agency, the National Hospital Organization, to operate these hospitals. This gave greater autonomy and flexibility to hospital management, which were no longer obliged to follow the civil administration regulation of government agencies restricting the hiring of personnel and in setting wages. The new governance structure demanded higher accountability from hospital directors, and permitted flexible labor contracts with hospital staff. These reforms collectively improved managerial accountability and efficiency among the national hospitals, and government subsidies are no longer required for operating the hospitals.

Although geographic disparities in distribution of physicians remain an issue, innovative approaches have been introduced, for example: prefectural governments subsidize the tuition and living expenses for the two to three entrants to the special medical school whose graduates are obligated to work in remote areas. The fee schedule has helped to mitigate the overconcentration of physicians in large urban hospitals and in specialized care by setting higher reimbursement rates for primary care services. It has also enabled hospitals in rural areas to offer higher salaries for doctors than those in urban areas to attract and retain them by paying them the same amount for the same service. By doing so, hospitals are able to offset the higher cost for physicians' salaries by offering lower salaries to nurses and other staff, who are willing to work for lower wages and are less likely to migrate to cities.

These experiences from Japan demonstrate that achieving and sustaining UHC is a complex process that requires long-term political commitment and continuous adjustments across many components of the health system that meet the changing social, economic, and demographic conditions of the country. The following chapters review the experiences of the 11 countries around the main themes of political economy, health financing, and human resources for health.

Notes

1. This section is summarized from the companion publication *Universal Health Coverage for Inclusive and Sustainable Development: Lessons from Japan* (Ikegami, forthcoming).

2. Fiscal space is defined as the available budget determined by a combination of the country's overall macroeconomic and fiscal context, public spending priorities, and how efficiently current expenditures are used.

Reference

Ikegami, N., ed. Forthcoming. *Universal Health Coverage for Inclusive and Sustainable Development: Lessons from Japan.* Washington, DC: World Bank.

CHAPTER 4

UHC Lessons in Political Economy and Policy Process

The international development community has recognized in recent years that carefully crafted technical solutions may have little practical effect if political economy concerns are ignored. The World Bank Group and other development agencies are increasingly acknowledging the importance of political economy and creating approaches to address related concerns in order to ensure that reforms in the health sector and beyond are enabled, rather than constrained (World Bank 2008; Poole 2011; Reich and Balarajan 2012).

The findings now presented synthesize themes that have emerged from consideration of the 11 country cases, and highlight the emerging lessons that are likely to be of interest and practical use to national policy makers.

Adopting UHC: Crises, Strong Leaders, and Social Movements All Contribute

Universal health coverage (UHC) initiatives are often adopted in response to a major social, economic, or political change. For example, UHC was adopted as a national priority following a financial crisis in Indonesia, Thailand, and Turkey (box 4.1); or at the time of redemocratization in Brazil; and as part of the postwar reconstruction effort in France and Japan. These moments of crisis or major upheaval offered opportunities for breaking through interest-group alignments that held back reforms, and allowed innovative approaches to be tested and adopted. They also served to mobilize the national solidarity needed to embark on such major reforms.

But crisis is not always needed to drive change. UHC may be adopted by a strong executive or political leadership. Equally, health care access enshrined in the constitution as a right has provided institutional underpinning to UHC initiatives in most of the 11 countries (Bangladesh, Brazil, France, Japan, Thailand, Turkey, and Vietnam), providing reformers with a legal basis for UHC advocacy. Other countries have relied on integrating UHC strategy within a national development plan to secure support and resources. Countries have also

Box 4.1 Financial Crisis as Impetus for Reform in Turkey

A crushing deficit, banking weakness, and capital flight led to a major economic crisis in Turkey in the early 2000s and prompted major government reform in the country, laying the basis for the 2003 Health Transformation Program. The aftermath of the financial crisis led to initiatives aimed at curtailing government deficits and creating leaner and more efficient state bureaucracies.

The reform-induced disruptions also created new opportunities for reforming health by breaking up old interest-group political arrangements. For example, they allowed the introduction of a new contracting mechanism with private providers through capitation payments that ushered in a more sustainable approach to health care provision, helping to make universal health coverage possible.

Sources: Akyuz and Boratav 2003; Tatar et al. 2011; Bump and Sparkes 2013.

Box 4.2 Social Movements for UHC in Brazil and Thailand

Prime ministers and political parties often get most of the credit for adopting universal health coverage (UHC) reforms, but social movements have also been crucial in helping to drive and support them. In Brazil and Thailand, for example, long-standing networks of doctors and public health professionals, concerned with expanding health equity and improving access to health care, put pressure on politicians to adopt universal coverage in moments of democratic change.

Brazil's *sanitarista* (public health) movement had long advocated for more equitable health reforms and played a critical role in institutionalizing principles of universalism in the 1988 constitution, following the transition to democracy in 1985, and for the 1990 Unified Health System Law. In Thailand, health care professionals who had worked in rural areas in the 1970s founded an organization called the Rural Doctors' Society that worked with grassroots partners in civil society to make expanding health care access an issue in the national elections in 2001. Once the ideas were adopted by a new political party, this movement was important subsequently in the implementation and governance of the new Universal Coverage Scheme.

Without these social movements, amid a backdrop of economic strain and competing policy priorities, UHC reforms in both these countries might have remained "on the shelf."

Sources: Weyland 1995; Falleti 2010; Harris 2012.

set explicit target dates for UHC as a way to mobilize political support and keep the country focused on the goal. These include Indonesia (with a target date of 2019), Vietnam (2020), and Bangladesh (2032).

In many countries, social movements helped put UHC on the political agenda initially and subsequently held governments accountable after it was adopted. Social movements and civil society have been especially important for helping to connect and engage important segments of the population with government and for protecting the interests of poor and vulnerable populations (box 4.2).

Economic growth, while instrumental in supporting the subsequent expansion of coverage, does not appear to have been a necessary condition for *adopting* the UHC agenda. Countries in Group 1 (Bangladesh and Ethiopia—see table 2.1), while facing significant macroeconomic constraints have still made UHC a national long-term goal. Brazil's commitment to UHC grew out of the redemocratization movement during a long period of slow economic growth. Thailand committed itself to expanding coverage under the Universal Coverage Scheme (UCS) in 2002, after the Asian financial crisis when macroeconomic growth prospects were still fragile. However, economic growth has been one of the important enabling factors underpinning the subsequent expansion of UHC in many countries once they adopted UHC. The recent expansion of coverage in Group 2 countries (Ghana, Indonesia, Peru, and Vietnam) has been aided by a relatively strong economic growth.

Achieving UHC: Incrementally and with Equity

All 11 countries have incrementally expanded UHC coverage, although they vary by aiming for single- or multiprogram coverage. Process complexity and the effort required to gain support among interest groups, as well as the time required to develop institutional and technical capacities, have demanded such incrementalism. Learning from past policy experiences—including mistakes—has proven invaluable for these countries, particularly those in Group 2, because they have made good progress but still face major gaps in coverage, and are reaching the stage where major review and adjustments are needed.

This incrementalism often leads to multiple risk pools, as different programs evolve to cover different population groups. This raises new challenges for ensuring equitable coverage and for redistributing resources across the pools which, once established, are politically difficult to merge or integrate, as this inevitably requires trade-offs, with some interest groups losing their privileges. Countries that have maintained multiple insurance programs (such as Japan) have had to develop a redistribution mechanism to allocate subsidies across the multiple plans to reduce inequities. But harmonizing benefits and contribution rates across the different groups has proven challenging and requires considerable political clout and leadership to enforce. All Group 2 countries have either made (Ghana and Vietnam) or are making (Indonesia and Peru) efforts to integrate or harmonize their multiple programs.

Expanding coverage to the informal sector is a major challenge for most low- and middle-income countries (LMICs), especially those doing so through contributory systems. The 11 country experiences show that countries tend to expand coverage first to civil servants or workers in the formal sector. Very frequently, this happens because those groups are often the easiest to cover and involve people who are politically active and live in urban areas that are near to existing health care infrastructure and who have institutionalized relationships with government through the payment of taxes. Households in the informal sector are thus excluded—and they are often the hardest groups to reach.

For the four Group 2 countries, expanding coverage to the informal sector remains a major challenge. Group 1 countries such as Bangladesh and Ethiopia are considering introducing social health insurance programs, which could result in steering government resources toward workers in the formal sector and away from less affluent farmers and informal sector workers.

Countries in Groups 3 and 4 have extended access to the poor and the informal sector through tax-funded approaches to subsidize their participation in a larger risk pool. Many countries in the process of expanding coverage toward UHC have created programs to provide free or subsidized coverage to the poor. However, these programs typically stand alongside a host of other programs that compete to cover different population groups and are subject to interest-group politics. Political leadership and social movements play an important role in ensuring that the resources to the poor are protected, especially in times of economic downturn. Even France only reached full UHC in 2000 when it introduced a state-subsidized program for low-income groups.

Evidence-based approaches that include a focus on community engagement appear important for successful implementation. In Bangladesh, the country's strong advances in health status—including life expectancy, fertility, and infant mortality—not only represent success, but also are instructive for the challenges that countries face along the path to UHC. Flexibility in policy, investment in innovation, and community engagement are three of the country's hallmarks.

Sustaining UHC: Responsive, Adaptive, and Resilient

Countries that have achieved UHC have learned from the shortcomings of their earlier policies, made adjustments, built on institutional and technical capacities, and tried different approaches without abandoning the guiding principles of UHC. Given the political, socioeconomic, and technical complexities of UHC, there is no unique right or wrong policy and no absolute success or failure. Policy makers' careful attention to the many factors—including governance structure, influences of lobbying groups, demographic and other socioeconomic changes, and global economic shifts—helps ensure that the health system responds to constantly changing population needs, technical innovations, and economic conditions. Adaptive leadership in Group 3 and 4 countries has been instrumental in directing such responses—especially at key points in the steps to UHC—which include taking into account the iterative nature of the process and recognizing that it takes time; learning lessons from experience and building on them; and mobilizing individuals and populations (Heifetz, Grashow, and Linsky 2009).

In this vein, Ghana is celebrating the 10th anniversary of establishing its National Health Insurance Scheme (NHIS), which integrated the earlier multiple community-based plans. The system is now at a turning point, with coverage hovering at 36 percent of the population and sustainability emerging as a major concern, as expenditure per beneficiary is outpacing revenues. Policy makers and executive managers of health care providers and the National Health Insurance Authority are reviewing the system and endeavoring to put it on a sustainable path. A similar review is under way in Vietnam, where the Ministry of Health and Vietnam Social Security (the health purchaser) have assessed the national health insurance system to propose consolidation adjustments for a revision to the Health Insurance Law. Indonesia is also moving to bring together multiple programs under an integrated national program. Peru passed legislation that makes it compulsory for public systems to exchange services.

Professional associations are important partners with the government in establishing and monitoring service quality licensure and standards, and serve as valuable resources for continuing education, thereby strengthening the capacity of clinicians to provide evidence-based practice services to more patients. Professional associations have also been influential in negotiating both for professional autonomy and the terms of compensation. In some cases, they have played a role in setting employment policies, for example by limiting the number of doctors or nurses who may practice, or setting conditions on the qualifications required to practice. Medical associations in Brazil, for example, have successfully lobbied to restrict nurses' scope of practice, and by setting these conditions for entering the health labor market they have influenced the overall availability and distribution of health workers.

Political leaders and policy makers need to understand the underlying political situation and negotiate with interest groups for ensuring equitable expansion. Professional bodies, labor unions, hospital and manufacturers' associations, and other interest groups influence basic decisions on allocating key inputs. Decisions on deployment of health workers, investment in infrastructure, and budgets for purchasing pharmaceuticals and supplies are often made by interest groups, and may not be aligned with UHC goals. Thus decision makers will need to include careful consideration of the political context, and plan to manage such politics. In Turkey, the leadership did just this (see box 4.3).

Box 4.3 The Importance of "Quick Wins" to Maintain Political Momentum—Experience from Turkey

At the time of the initiation of Turkey's Health Transformation Program, nearly 25 million people lacked access or had limited access to health care, amounting to approximately 36 percent of the population. Thinking strategically about how to consolidate support among that population played an important role in balancing the challenges posed by urban elites and organized interests. Turkey's reform team recognized the need to enact visible positive changes in order to win public support and secure political support for continued reform efforts very early on. The Ministry of Health therefore acted quickly, targeting areas with the fewest services. It added coverage for outpatient services in its Green Card program in 2004 and for outpatient medicines in 2005 (Aran and Rokx, forthcoming).

Even more visibly, the reformers acted immediately to abolish the unpopular practice of holding patients in medical facilities who were delinquent in paying their bills. They also reorganized and expanded space for delivering care in primary health care facilities and increased

box continues next page

Universal Health Coverage for Inclusive and Sustainable Development
http://dx.doi.org/10.1596/978-1-4648-0297-3

Box 4.3 The Importance of "Quick Wins" to Maintain Political Momentum—Experience from Turkey *(continued)*

emergency transportation services by three- to five-fold in the first 10 years, including the number of ambulances and aircraft that served remote areas. These changes served as powerful and visible reminders of the government's concern for the people and contributed to improved service delivery and patient satisfaction: the percentage of people reporting problems making an appointment was halved in just two years, while satisfaction with health services jumped measurably over the first two years of the reform and to nearly 76 percent by 2011. These changes not only improved the political standing of the Health Transformation Program but also helped the AK Party to build on its majority in 2007 and 2011 general elections, helping to maintain political momentum for sustained reform (Bump and Sparkes 2013).

References

Akyuz, Y., and K. Boratav. 2003. "The Making of the Turkish Financial Crisis." *World Development* 31 (9): 1549–66.

Aran, M., and C. Rokx. Forthcoming. "Turkey on the Way of Universal Health Coverage through the Health Transformation Program (2003–2013)." World Bank, Washington, DC.

Bump, J., and S. Sparkes. 2013. *A Political Economy Analysis of Turkey's Health Transformation Program*. Washington, DC: World Bank.

Falleti, T. 2010. "Infiltrating the State: The Evolution of Health Care Reforms in Brazil, 1964–1988." In *Explaining Institutional Change: Ambiguity, Agency, and Power*, edited by J. Mahoney and K. Thelen. New York: Cambridge University Press.

Harris, J. 2012. "A Right to Health? Professional Networks, HIV/AIDS, and the Politics of Universal Healthcare." PhD dissertation, University of Wisconsin-Madison.

———. 2013. "Uneven Inclusion: Consequences of Universal Healthcare in Thailand." *Citizenship Studies* 17 (1): 111–27.

Heifetz, R., A. Grashow, and M. Linsky. 2009. *The Theory behind the Practice: A Brief Introduction to the Adaptive Leadership Framework*. Boston: Harvard Business Press.

Ikegami, N., ed. Forthcoming. *Universal Health Coverage for Inclusive and Sustainable Development: Lessons from Japan*. Washington, DC: World Bank.

Poole, A. 2011. *How-To Notes: Political Economy Assessments at Sector and Project Levels*. Washington, DC: World Bank.

Reich, M. R., and Y. Balarajan. 2012. *Political Economy Analysis for Food and Nutrition Security*. Washington, DC: World Bank and South Asia Food and Nutrition Security Initiative (SAFANSI).

Tatar, M., S. Mollahaliloğlu, B. Şahin, S. Aydın, A. Maresso, and C. Hernández-Quevedo. 2011. "Turkey: Health System Review." *Health Systems in Transition* 13 (6).

Weyland, K. 1995. "Social Movements and the State: The Politics of Health Reform in Brazil." *World Development* 23 (10): 1699–712.

World Bank. 2008. *The Political Economy of Policy Reform: Issues and Implications for Policy Dialogue and Development Operations*. Washington, DC: World Bank.

CHAPTER 5

UHC Lessons in Health Financing

A pledge to achieve universal health coverage (UHC) requires the government both to make a fiscal commitment and to play a leading role in establishing pooling and redistributive mechanisms. No country has in fact reached UHC relying solely on private voluntary sources (Kutzin 2012). Health financing mechanisms also require careful regulation and management to ensure equity, fiscal responsibility, and value for money. A 2007 review by the Organisation for Economic Co-operation and Development (OECD) of private health insurance in low- and middle-income countries (LMICs; Drechsler and Jütting 2007) showed that its role varied by economic, social, and institutional setting. Such insurance programs can be valuable when complementing existing financing options, but only if they are carefully managed, regulated, and adapted to local needs and preferences. Health services themselves are highly susceptible to market failure, due to difficulties in measuring and accounting for the use of resources and their impact on quality, safety, and effectiveness, which makes the task of financing health care that much more complex.

The following sections describe key themes and lessons from the 11 case studies in addressing these challenges.

Raising Revenues

All 11 countries have problems finding the fiscal space to finance UHC policies and programs sustainably, but the nature of the problem varies. Countries in Group 1—those with the fewest resources—face macroeconomic constraints and limited government capacity to raise revenues. They rely on external assistance to finance many health benefits, and a major issue is leveraging external assistance in a way that complements the country's own budget contributions and supports its own policy priorities. Bangladesh, for example, has a Sector-wide Approach to harmonize external assistance, and Ethiopia is directing external assistance to finance investments—in infrastructure, equipment, and supplies—that supplement its own budget for salaries of health workers.

Countries in Group 2 are middle-income countries beginning to benefit from strong macroeconomic growth and an expanding fiscal space, although budget commitments for health vary. Ghana and Peru each allocated just over 9 percent of their total government budget on health in 2012, and both countries recorded around 4.8 percent of GDP on total health expenditures in 2011. But health coverage was very different for the two countries in 2012: 36 percent for Ghana and 62 percent for Peru (a sharp gain over its 53 percent in 2008).

Vietnam raised its share of government health budget commitments from 6.3 percent of the total government budget in 2002 to 9.4 percent in 2011, or 2.7 percent of GDP. Over the same period, its real gross national income per capita nearly doubled, and population health coverage expanded from 16 percent to nearly 68 percent. Thus Vietnam is an example where government spending on health grew faster than economic output. Much of this increase was used to subsidize premiums for health insurance among the poor. Indonesia's health budget, by contrast, has remained relatively low over the past two decades.

Figure 5.1 highlights the 11 governments' spending on health as a share of GDP. Figure 5.2 shows government spending on health as a share of the total government budget for Group 2 countries, and figure 5.3 for Group 3 countries.

Figure 5.1 Government Spending on Health as a Percentage of GDP, 2011

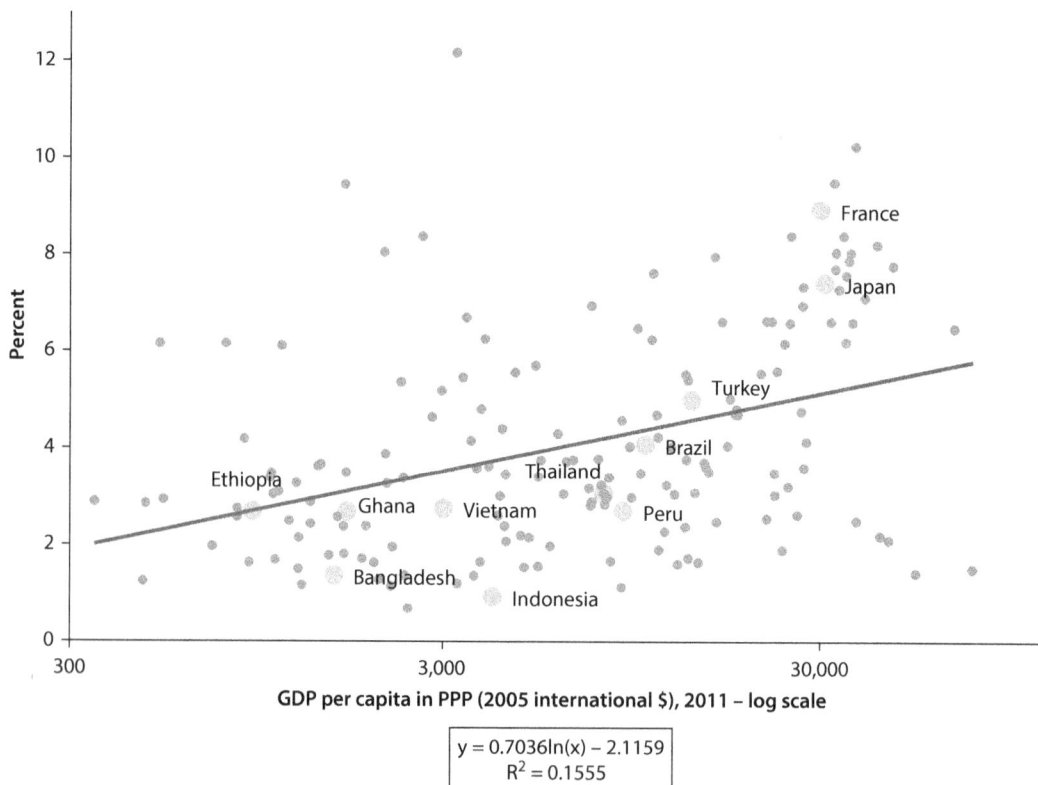

$$y = 0.7036\ln(x) - 2.1159$$
$$R^2 = 0.1555$$

Source: WDI 2013.
Note: The 11 case study countries are highlighted. GDP = gross domestic product; PPP = purchasing power parity.

Figure 5.2 Government Spending on Health as a Percentage of Total Government Expenditure, Group 2 Countries, 1995–2012

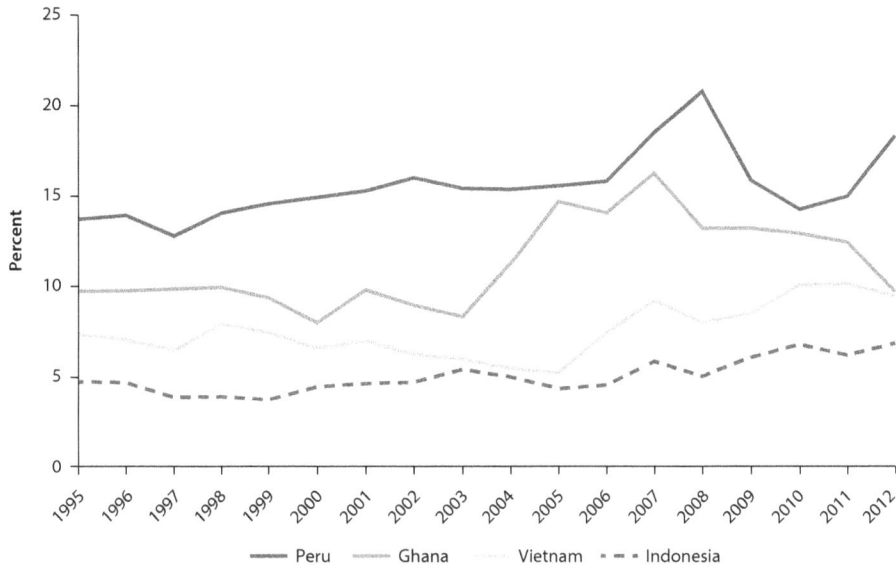

Source: World Health Organization National Health Accounts database, www.who.int/health-accounts.

Figure 5.3 Government Spending on Health as a Percentage of Total Government Expenditure, Group 3 Countries, 1995–2012

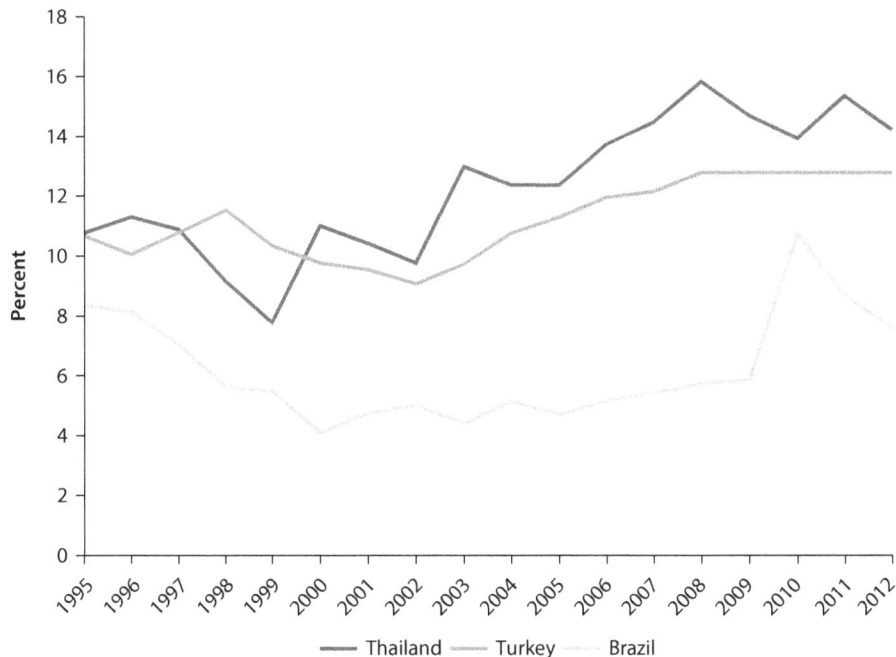

Source: World Health Organization National Health Accounts database, www.who.int/health-accounts.

Universal Health Coverage for Inclusive and Sustainable Development
http://dx.doi.org/10.1596/978-1-4648-0297-3

Priority in the government budget for health, with macroeconomic growth, has been important in enabling countries to expand population coverage and provide better financial protection (table 5.1), although few governments accompany their political commitment to UHC with an explicit financial pledge—only Brazil, France, and Ghana earmark revenue (table 5.2). Others that have achieved UHC have done so without this approach but have consistently kept their health allocation relatively high. In Japan, for example, the Ministry of Finance and the Ministry of Health, Labour and Welfare negotiate to set the fiscal subsidy each year, and the fee schedule and payment systems are adjusted every two years (Ikegami, forthcoming). Thailand and Turkey have generally had good macroeconomic conditions and placed a high priority on health in the budget.

Table 5.1 Macro/Fiscal Conditions in UHC in Case Study Countries during Rapid Expansion of Health Coverage

Country	Period of rapid population coverage expansion[a]	Income classification at the end of the period or currently[a]	Change in population coverage (%)	Change in GNI per capita[b]		Change in government share of THE[a] (%)	Change in health share in government budget[a] (%)
				Nominal ($)	Real (%)		
Group 2: Coverage expansion							
Ghana	2003–present	Lower-middle	6.6–38.0	320–1,550	45	41.0–56.1	8.7–11.9
Indonesia	2004–present	Lower-middle	28–41[c]	1,090–3,420	74	39.5–34.1	5.0–5.3
Peru	2003–present	Upper-middle	36.8–62.0	2,160–6,060	79	58.7–56.1	15.4–15.0
Vietnam	2002–present	Lower-middle	16.0–67.5	430–1,550	82	30.5–40.3	6.3–9.4
Group 3: Deepening coverage							
Brazil	1988–2000	Upper-middle	50–100	2,250–3,860	41	43.0–40.3	N/A–4.1 (8.7 in 2011)
Thailand	2001–06	Lower-middle	63–96	1,900–2,890	41	56.4–72.7	10.4–13.4 (14.5 in 2011)
Turkey	2002–12	Upper-middle	64–98	3,480–10,830	111	70.7–74.9	9.1–12.9
Group 4: Maintenance and new challenges							
France	1945–78	High	N/A–100	N/A	453	N/A	N/A (15.9 in 2011)
Japan	1945–61	Middle	70–100	N/A	229	N/A	N/A (18.2 in 2011)

Note: GNI = gross national income; N/A = not available; THE = total health expenditure; UHC = universal health coverage.

a. **Ghana:** 2003, National Health Insurance Law (Act 650) passed. Expansion has stalled since 2010.
Indonesia: 2004, *Jamkesmas* government-funded insurance program for the poor introduced. Expansion has stalled since 2010.
Peru: 2003, Seguro Integral de Salud (Integrated Health Insurance, or SIS) introduced to cover the poor and the informal sector. Expansion continues.
Vietnam: 2002, introduction of Health Care Fund for the Poor. Expansion continues.
Brazil: 1988, health established as a right in the constitution and the Sistema Único de Saúde (Unified Health System, or SUS) was set up. UHC was considered achieved in 2000 when the Family Health Strategy fully implemented expanding primary care coverage.
Thailand: 2001, launch of Universal Coverage Scheme (UCS). Universal coverage reached in 2006.
Turkey: 2003, Health Transformation Program initiated (2002–12 referenced in UHC country summary report for Turkey).
France: 1945, General Social Security system adopted. In 1961, insurance was extended to farmers, in 1966 to the self-employed, in 1978 to uncovered workers, and in 2000 to the remaining uncovered population.
Japan: 1961, the last municipalities established community insurance programs when enrollment became compulsory for all.
b. WDI 2013.
c. Harimurti et al. 2013.

Table 5.2 Financial Earmarking and Commitments to UHC in the 11 Countries

Political commitment to UHC accompanied by earmarking	France	Earmarked taxes (initially payroll tax; since 1998 earmarked taxes on income and capital)
	Ghana	Earmarked portion of value-added tax and social security contributions
	Brazil	The minimum to be allocated to the Ministry of Health and to state and municipal health secretariats is defined by Constitutional Amendment No. 29/2000[a]
Political commitment without earmarked commitment	Japan	No earmarked amounts, but high priority in the budget
	Thailand	
	Turkey	
	Vietnam	
	Bangladesh	No earmarked amounts, and varying priority in the budget
	Ethiopia	
	Indonesia	
	Peru	

Sources: Summarized from the 11 UHC country summary reports, http://www.worldbank.org/en/topic/health/brief/uhc-japan.
a. To the Ministry of Health, the equivalent of the health budget from the previous fiscal year adjusted by the nominal change in GDP; to states, 12 percent of the budget; and to municipalities, 15 percent of the budget.
Note: GDP = gross domestic product; UHC = universal health coverage.

Brazil integrated its multiple programs into a single publicly funded Unified Health System (SUS) covering the whole population, financed through general taxation. Private health insurance is permitted in the constitution, so it remained part of the system, although it was expected to be supplemental to SUS. Low health budgets and SUS underfunding led both the private service sector and private health insurance programs to expand. Although the whole population is entitled to free services in the SUS system, the chronic underfunding has driven many to the private market with a concurrent growth in private insurance. Consequently, financial protection has eroded and out-of-pocket spending has increased, and at 30 percent, Brazil has the highest share of out-of-pocket spending among Group 3 and 4 countries (figure 5.4). Private spending is concentrated among the wealthiest, with the top income quintile accounting for 58 percent (private insurance and out-of-pocket payments combined), but it also places a burden on low-income households, consuming up to 7 percent of their income (Uga and Santos 2007).

In France and Japan, demographic changes (such as an aging population and a decline in the share of working-age adults), combined with prolonged recession, have curtailed fiscal space. Thus these two Group 4 countries are now seeking ways to diversify their revenue base, including raising the consumption tax (which Japan did in early April 2014, increasing the sales tax from 5 percent to 8 percent; it will rise again, to 10 percent, in October 2015) and further diversifying earmarked taxes (France). In France, wage-based contributions constituted 98 percent of the total at the inception of the social health insurance system in 1945, but now represent less than half. Unemployment was another factor in lowering wage-based contributions in that country.

Other countries are also seeking to diversify revenue sources, and strategies often vary by stage of UHC: countries with a large informal sector such

Figure 5.4 Out-of-Pocket Health Spending as a Percentage of Total Health Expenditure, 2011

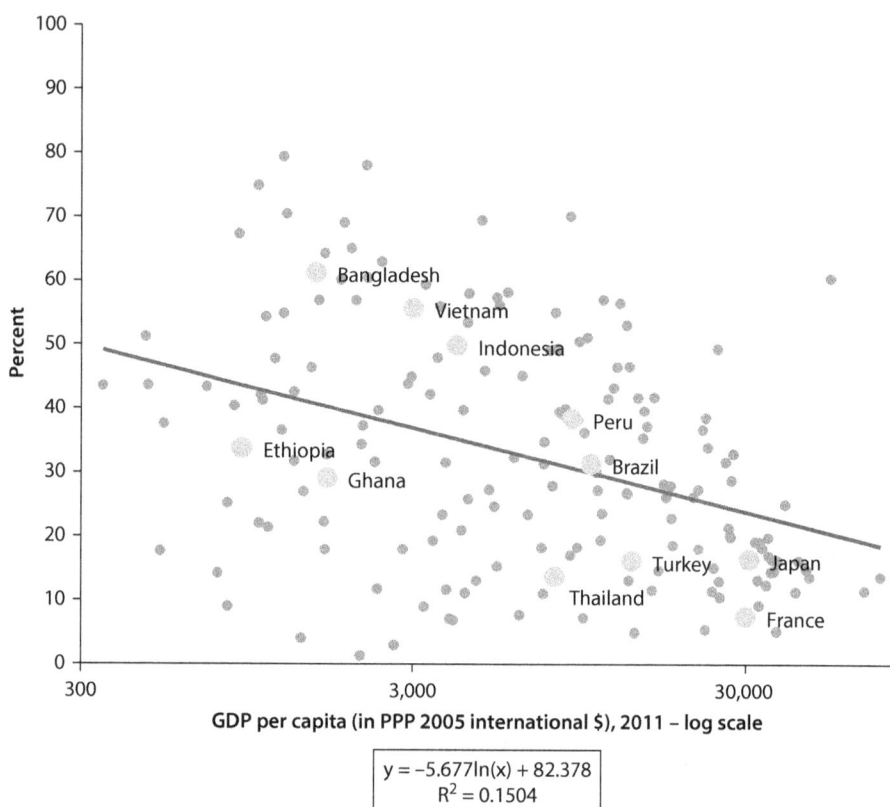

$$y = -5.677\ln(x) + 82.378$$
$$R^2 = 0.1504$$

Source: WDI 2013.
Note: The 11 country case studies are highlighted. GDP = gross domestic product; PPP = purchasing power parity.

as Thailand and Vietnam have also found it hard to expand coverage through payroll taxes alone and have expanded their allocation to health through general revenues. By contrast, low-income countries such as Bangladesh and Ethiopia are seeking ways to expand their narrow tax base by introducing new payroll taxes under a social insurance program.

Managing Expenditures Well and Ensuring Value for Money

As all countries face resource constraints in achieving or sustaining universal coverage, managing spending efficiently is critical. Countries therefore need to set up (or fine-tune) expenditure management policies and systems that ensure that the expansion of coverage can provide benefits in a fiscally disciplined and accountable manner. Fiscal sustainability of the health system means that health expenditure growth does not exceed available resources, which are determined by the fiscal context and policy priorities.

Countries at early stages of UHC have to mobilize resources to expand coverage, a move that relies on increases in health expenditure. These countries have tended to focus more on mobilizing revenues to expand coverage and less on managing costs. Cost pressures always emerge, however, as coverage expands. Often, policies borne from compromises early in the design and adoption phase, such as fee-for-service payment to gain the buy-in of providers, plant the seeds of future cost escalation. Weak attention to expenditure management in early stages can potentially leave countries vulnerable to cost escalation and subsequent strong policy influence by interest groups later. Thus investing in the institutional capacity to use expenditure management during the design phase and at key junctures of system refinement is important for enabling future coverage expansion.

In addition to natural sources of cost pressure in the health system such as aging populations, advances in medical technology, and rising demand for more and better services as incomes grow, policy choices in UHC system design also affect the pace of cost growth. In particular, countries relying on open-ended fee-for-service payment face challenges with cost escalation. Various countries in Groups 1, 2, and 4 either pay providers open-ended fee for service (Ethiopia, France, Ghana, and Indonesia) or have ineffective caps (Peru and Vietnam). In Peru for instance, one of the main social health insurance funds (Seguro Integral de Salud, SIS) pays providers open-ended fee for service with, ostensibly, no budget caps, but to stay within the budget regional administrators impose implicit caps by ceasing to provide certain services, medicines, tests, or procedures (Francke 2013). Similarly in Vietnam the health purchaser, Vietnam Social Security, pays most hospitals by fee for service with a global budget cap, but there are strong incentives for hospitals to spend beyond the cap, since Vietnam Social Security typically reimburses hospitals up to 60 percent of their overruns. Overspending in one year leads to a higher cap the next, which in turn results in a more generous budget over time.

How expenditure management is carried out is critical, as simply pursuing cost containment may erode coverage. Expenditures must be managed carefully to improve efficiency in a way that leads, on balance, to coverage-enhancing outcomes. Examples of coverage-eroding cost-containment measures include an increase in cost sharing and a shift to beneficiaries of the financial burden, thereby increasing informal payments and eroding financial protection. In Brazil for instance, the chronic underfinancing of SUS has led to limited access to high-quality health services for lower-income groups, while wealthier households have private insurance.

Finding the right mix of policies that help contain unnecessary cost growth without eroding coverage (even while overall spending may need to increase) is tricky, although experience from countries in Groups 3 and 4 may offer suggestions. These countries typically use a mix of expenditure targets, strategic purchasing, and emphasis on cost-effective primary care (table 5.3).

France sets explicit national spending targets, with rigorous monitoring to help keep expenditures within them. It has recently introduced pay-for-performance

Table 5.3 Coverage-Enhancing Expenditure Management Approaches

France	• A set of expenditure controls through prospective and compulsory spending targets; primary care gatekeeping strengthened; pay for performance for general practitioners introduced; and the hospital payment system reformed
Japan	• Nationally managed fee schedule revised every two years to keep total expenditure increases within agreed level of budget subsidies set by government
Thailand	• Closed-ended capitation contracting with diagnosis-related group hospital payment • Strong primary care gatekeeping • Tough negotiations with pharmaceutical companies • Priority setting for expanding the benefits package • System focused on primary care
Turkey	• Closed-ended payment systems with performance-based component (global budget for hospitals and capitation for primary care) • Expenditure caps at hospital level and on pharmaceuticals • System focused on primary care

Sources: Summarized from the universal health coverage country summary reports on France, Japan, Thailand, and Turkey, http://www .worldbank.org/en/topic/health/brief/uhc-japan.

contracts for primary care (initially paid fee for service) as a means to control costs while simultaneously improving quality and coordination of care—although the outcomes of these efforts have yet to be evaluated. Japan has a unique approach that uses its fee-for-service system as a way to meet expenditure targets through its biennial revision of the fee schedule, which places strong downward pressure on total health spending. The country offers financial protection to households by capping copayments and subsidizing catastrophic health expenditures, mea- sures that have helped it mitigate the coverage-eroding effects of an open-ended fee-for-service payment system.

Some Group 3 and 4 countries have introduced policies that use strategic purchasing to reduce rents accumulating to interest groups, such as tertiary care providers and pharmaceutical companies, rather than cutting back benefits. Here, a strong purchasing agency with the leverage and capacity to negotiate prices with providers and suppliers on behalf of beneficiaries can help manage costs without eroding coverage, as exemplified in Thailand and Turkey's integration of health programs. Thailand's National Health Security Office is the single purchaser for three-quarters of the country's population under the Universal Coverage Scheme (UCS; with about 50 million beneficiaries). It has negotiated down prices of medicines, medical products, and interventions—cutting, for example, the price of hemodialysis from $67 to $50 per cycle, potentially saving $170 million a year (Health Insurance System Research Office 2012).

Two other types of expenditure management stand out. Some countries have focused on supply-side policies that promote more cost-effective interventions, including investments in primary care and public health functions, and stronger regulation when new technologies are brought in. They have also used demand- side management, including strategic copayments to discourage unnecessary services or to encourage utilization of primary care, or have offered incentives and subsidies to patients for services with public health benefits.

Countries more successful in managing costs without eroding coverage have used a mix of different approaches. In Thailand and Turkey, policies include a balanced approach to prioritizing services and medicines for benefits package expansion, strong negotiation with pharmaceutical companies, and leveraging provider payment systems to bring more benefits to more people. In France, 20 years of health-budget deficits have started to decline in the past few years through a series of reforms including national spending targets, provider payments for primary and acute care, and tighter state stewardship on health insurance spending through rigorous monitoring. The problem is far from being solved, however, as the economic downturn has put further strain on budget revenues, and new cost pressures have arisen.

Managing Risk Pooling and Redistribution of Resources

Providing UHC and financial protection for the whole population requires cross-subsidization, both from rich to poor and from people at low risk of illness (such as the young) to people with higher risk (such as the elderly). The structure of UHC programs as well as the sequencing of coverage expansion are critical for redistribution to achieve equity.

Although the appropriate structure of risk pooling is specific to the country context, cross-subsidization appears to be more effective when there is a single integrated program based on general tax revenue. Turkey has done this and achieved a high degree of cross-subsidization and equity in financing. Although Ghana has yet to achieve universal coverage, within the risk pool established under the National Health Insurance Scheme (NHIS), redistribution from wealthy to poorer households has been largely achieved, made possible by progressive general taxes for most funding in the system, as well as the redistributive function of the NHIS pool. One study on Ghana found that the poorest 20 percent of households bear less than 3 percent of the burden of funding the system, but the wealthiest 20 percent almost 60 percent (Akazili, Gyapong, and McIntyre 2011).

Risk pooling and cross-subsidization constitute a major challenge, however, when coverage expands through multiple programs. Thailand's UCS (with the most beneficiaries in the country) ensures cross-subsidization and equitable financial risk protection within this group. However, the country still has three separate insurance programs, and annual per-beneficiary expenditure across them is highly skewed because of lack of redistribution: in 2011, $366 for the Civil Servant Scheme, $97 for the UCS, and $71 for the Formal Sector Program.

Some countries have achieved cross-subsidization with multiple programs by standardizing key facets of the system and cross-subsidizing or consolidating pools. Group 4 countries have achieved this over multiple programs by standardizing the benefits package and enforcing redistribution mechanisms (Japan) or consolidating into fewer programs with larger pools (France). Japan uses a combination of standardization of benefits and provider payment across plans, intergovernmental transfers of subsidies, as well as transfers between funds.

For example, in 2013 the insurance programs for large corporations were expected to transfer about 46 percent of the premiums they collect directly to the programs enrolling elders. This transfer is on top of the general revenue subsidies going to these programs. Cross-subsidization has not, however, kept pace with the changing demographic profile, and disparities in premium rates are growing among the social health insurance groups.

Consolidating insurance programs has been key to expanding coverage equitably in several countries. Among those in Group 3, Turkey, for example, undertook major reforms to achieve this as well as integration and cross-subsidization. Brazil's 1988 constitution established the SUS, financed through general taxation. Thailand consolidated two programs in 2001, but still maintains three separate programs (as just seen). Among Group 2 countries, Ghana and Vietnam have integrated several programs: Ghana has a single risk pool under its National Health Insurance Law; in Vietnam, however, the actual pooling of revenues and cross-subsidization of expenditures remain incomplete. Indonesia and Peru are moving to consolidate multiple programs in a final push to UHC. Indonesia launched the National Health Insurance program (JKN) officially on January 1, 2014, which will become the single-payer umbrella covering all citizens, integrating programs previously covered by the government and other social insurance programs. In Peru, the 2010 Universal Health Insurance Law created a regulatory framework to achieve UHC through a coordinated institutional integration process of the two main social insurance funds (SIS and EsSalud). Peru is working on plans for further institutional integration.

Several countries started with small-scale risk-pooling mechanisms using community-based health insurance (CBHI). International evidence has shown that CBHI programs typically contribute only a little to improving revenue generation, risk pooling, and financial protection (Carrin, Waelkens, and Criel 2005), partly because of their voluntary nature, inability to generate sufficient revenue to offer an attractive benefits package, and lack of trust and accountability. In Ghana and Japan, however, CBHI programs were brought under the financing and policy umbrella of national systems and served as a useful step toward UHC. In both countries, government subsidies allowed the programs to reach a larger population and offer a more generous benefits package. Japan made participation mandatory, thereby fully incorporating CBHI into the national health insurance system.

Countries also aim to improve cross-subsidization, equity, and financial protection through targeted subsidies and exemptions. Using different mechanisms, all 11 countries provide subsidies for coverage, services, or cost sharing for the poor and other priority groups—or all three (table 5.4).

Group 1 countries focus the subsidies on fee waivers or vouchers for the poor for services provided in public facilities. Group 2 countries have contributory insurance programs with public subsidies directed to cover premiums for the poor and other priority groups. When choosing targeting mechanisms, policy makers often accept leakage of subsidies to the nonpoor as the cost to pay for minimizing undercoverage, but even then many individuals entitled to premium exemptions are not covered.

Table 5.4 Subsidies Targeting the Poor

Country	Targeting of subsidies and exemptions
Group 1	
Bangladesh	A voucher program entitles women to access free antenatal care, delivery care, emergency referral, postpartum care services, and cash stipends to cover transportation costs and purchases of nutritious foods and medicines.
Ethiopia	A new fee waiver system is being introduced for poor households, selected through community participation.
Group 2	
Ghana	Poor and vulnerable groups are exempt from paying NHIS premiums, which are subsidized through the value-added tax's earmarked portion. Exempt groups include all seniors aged 70 and above, retirees who contributed to the social security program, children under 18, pregnant women, and indigents. Overall, 65–68 percent of members fall into one of the exempt groups. A high degree of leakage of the subsidy to the nonpoor is suspected, with many exempt individuals not enrolled.
Indonesia	Coverage for the poor and near-poor by *Jamkesmas* is subsidized by general revenues. The poor and near-poor are identified by a combination of means testing and local-government eligibility criteria. Widespread deficient targeting and leakages (>50 percent) to the nonpoor stem from variable eligibility criteria and lack of validated targeting. The *Jampersal* program provides free maternity services (prenatal, delivery, and postnatal) to all pregnant women, regardless of income.
Peru	Enrollment in SIS is subsidized for the poor and near-poor with general revenue funds. Leakage to the nonpoor is significant.
Vietnam	The government fully subsidizes health insurance premiums for children under 6, the elderly, and the poor, and partly subsidizes premiums for the near-poor and students. The poor are identified through local targeting that includes an economic survey and voting among community leaders.
Group 3	
Brazil	A subsidized health care system is available to all citizens, but some implicit targeting occurs as wealthier individuals choose additional private coverage.
Thailand	With a noncontributory system, all coverage is financed through general tax revenues (except the Formal Sector Program).
Turkey	Individuals are classified into one of four income groups. Premiums are fully subsidized for the lowest income group, and are on a sliding scale for the other three.
Group 4	
France	A state-subsidized program, with no copayments, operates for low-income groups, providing the standard insured benefits package. An extended benefits package (including complementary coverage as a substitute for private insurance) covers the poorest. Targeted subsidies apply for chronic diseases, and financial incentives (subsidized vouchers) for accessing private voluntary health insurance.
Japan	Premiums of the elderly, self-employed, and unemployed enrolled in municipality-managed programs are highly subsidized through transfers from central and local government, and from other risk pools with fewer elders.

Sources: Synthesized from the 11 UHC country summary reports, http://www.worldbank.org/en/topic/health/brief/uhc-japan.
Note: NHIS = National Health Insurance Scheme; SIS = Seguro Integral de Salud; UHC = universal health coverage.

Effective targeting is often a challenge in the absence of identification systems and in some cases even definitions of the poor. Ghana is piloting a unified targeting mechanism for all social assistance programs, which also will be adopted to target premium subsidies in the NHIS. Ethiopia and Vietnam rely on community-based approaches to identify the poor. Several countries (including Bangladesh, Ghana, and Indonesia) target specific services such as maternity care for subsidies and exemptions, regardless of income.

References

Akazili, J., J. Gyapong, and D. McIntyre. 2011. "Who Pays for Health Care in Ghana?" *International Journal for Equity in Health* 10: 26.

Carrin, G., M. Waelkens, and B. Criel. 2005. "Community-Based Health Insurance in Developing Countries: A Study of Its Contribution to the Performance of Health Financing Systems." *Tropical Medicine and International Health* 10 (8): 799–811.

Drechsler, D., and J. Jütting. 2007. "Different Countries, Different Needs: The Role of Private Health Insurance in Developing Countries." *Journal of Health Politics, Policy and Law* 32 (3): 497–534.

Francke, P. 2013. "Peru's Comprehensive Health Insurance and New Challenges for Universal Coverage." UNICO Studies Series 11, World Bank, Washington, DC.

Harimurti, P., E. Pambudi, A. Pigazzini, and A. Tandon. 2013. "The Nuts and Bolts of Jamkesmas, Indonesia's Government-Financed Health Coverage Program for the Poor and Near-Poor." UNICO Case Study, Health, Nutrition, and Population Unit, World Bank, Washington, DC.

Health Insurance System Research Office. 2012. *Thailand's Universal Coverage Scheme: Achievements and Challenges. An Independent Assessment of the First 10 Years (2001–2010).* Nonthaburi, Thailand.

Ikegami, N., ed. Forthcoming. *Universal Health Coverage for Inclusive and Sustainable Development: Lessons from Japan.* Washington, DC: World Bank.

Kutzin, J. 2012. "Anything Goes on the Path to Universal Health Coverage? No." *Bulletin of the World Health Organization* 90: 867–68.

Uga, M., and I. Santos. 2007. "An Analysis of Equity in Brazilian Health System Financing." *Health Affairs* 26 (4): 1017–28.

WDI (World Development Indicators). 2013. http://data.worldbank.org/data-catalog/world-development-indicators.

CHAPTER 6

UHC Lessons in Human Resources for Health

Improving access to health services—whether in the form of essential medicines and technologies to prevent health problems or to diagnose and treat patients—requires well-trained and motivated health workers. The 11 countries face disparate challenges in health worker production, distribution, and performance for meeting their changing health care needs.

Increasing the Production of Qualified Health Workers

The expansion of benefits and coverage under universal health coverage (UHC) requires investments in the health workforce to ensure affordable, appropriate, and effective health services. Countries that have committed to UHC face increasing pressures to increase the production of health workers to meet growing and changing demand for health services in the public and private sectors—the latter including for-profit and community-based nonprofit entities.

Health worker shortages are a global issue, but are especially acute for countries in the early stages of UHC adoption and achievement. Of the 11, those in Groups 1, 2, and 3 are at various stages in their efforts to scale up education and training (table 6.1). While criticisms have been raised over the viability of the threshold estimate, the approach has helped draw attention to the global health workforce crisis. These figures are not meant to inform decision makers about an optimal distribution of health workers in their country nor to establish a normative standard, but rather offer an indication of the size of the task facing low-income countries. Bangladesh and Ethiopia, for example, with a 4- to 13-fold increase in their skilled health professionals—even when spread over two decades—face a daunting challenge, suggesting that they and other countries in the early stages of UHC need to revisit traditional models of education, deployment, and remuneration.

Thus scaling up production is not only about adding new staff, but requires analysis of the current workforce profile and skills mix to match the prevailing

Table 6.1 Health Workforce Estimates for the 11 Countries, c. 2010 and Targets for 2035

Country	Density of skilled health professionals (doctors, nurses, and midwives) per 10,000 population, c. 2010	Percentage change in workforce required to reach 22.8 threshold[a] by 2035
Group 1		
Bangladesh	5.7	404
Ethiopia	2.7	1,354
Group 2		
Ghana	13.6	221
Indonesia	16.1	78
Peru	22.2	33
Vietnam	22.3	19[b]
Group 3		
Brazil	81.4	0
Thailand	17.4	32
Turkey	41.1	0
Group 4		
France	126.6	0
Japan	63.3	0

Source: GHWA and WHO 2013.
a. Health workforce density of 22.8 skilled health professionals per 10,000 population is the lower level recommended by the World Health Organization to achieve relatively high coverage for essential health interventions in countries most in need (WHO 2006).
b. Authors' calculation.

labor market conditions as well as service requirements (McPake et al. 2013). The 11 countries have considerable variation in this skills mix, in categories of professionals (doctors, nurses, midwives, community health workers) and within professional groups (generalists and specialist doctors) (figure 6.1). They also have very different skills mixes—and globally there are a wide variation and no clear indication of a universal optimal mix. However, a highly skewed mix—for example, countries with a very high ratio of doctors to nurses, as in Bangladesh—means that doctors may not be working optimally because they may have to cover for the paucity of nurses. Countries should examine their current skills mix, benchmark against others, and make policy decisions about the need for any adjustment to improve UHC attainment.

Broadening the recruitment pool and offering flexible career opportunities to health workers will be important for expanding the health workforce in a relatively short time. Many low- and middle-income countries (LMICs) have a shallow pool of graduates while the demand for health professionals outstrips their production capacity. High-income countries face similar challenges in recruiting students at a time when demand for health and long-term care continues to rise. To address this gap, many countries are introducing mechanisms to broaden the recruitment pool, and are examining flexible and nontraditional routes into the health workforce.

Some of the 11 countries are expanding recruitment of mid- and lower-level health workers, and in some cases creating new categories of health workers to

Figure 6.1 Ratio of Nurses and Midwives to Doctors

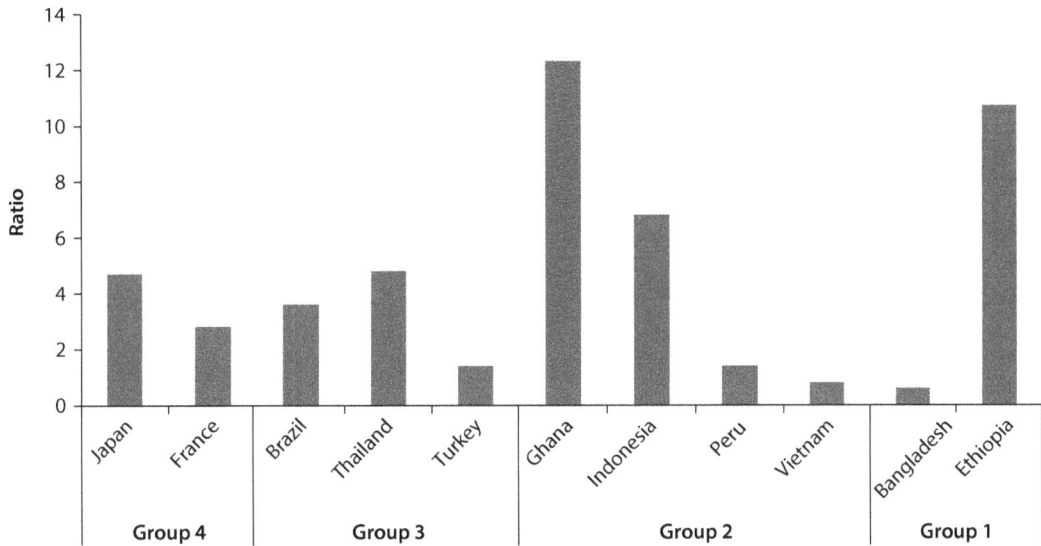

Sources: WDI (2013 or latest year available); for Japan, Ministry of Health, Labour and Welfare for Japan.

meet the needs of communities. These workers have shorter periods of education and can be developed and deployed faster. Examples include Ethiopia's health extension workers (box 6.1), Brazil's community health workers, and Japan's licensed practical nurses (Ikegami, forthcoming). These strategies have helped greatly in expanding health services by building up the workforce capacity in underserved areas or specialties. However, they also require multiple changes in the way health care is delivered and a redefinition of the scope of practice and functions of health worker categories. They frequently also require the system of regulation to be developed further, so as to set the various levels of education content, as well as standards of training and practice. Regulation should clearly distinguish the scope of practice of different categories, so as to avoid role confusion or unnecessary role overlap, and to ensure safe care provision.

Countries that want to scale up their health workforce will need better estimates of the time required to develop and deploy different staff types, and of their costs and options for achieving optimum staffing and mix within their available labor and resource pools. They will also need to understand job and labor market conditions that these workers will face and the incentives influencing workers' choices and their willingness to take up employment to achieve a better match between job characteristics and workers' preferences. For the most effective investments, policy makers and managers in the public and private sectors will require information on the labor markets in the health sector generally, as well as specific issues such as the relative costs of employing different types of staff, their scope of practice to ensure the best possible impact on care access, quality, and outcomes of these types, and the appropriate educational

Box 6.1 Ethiopia's Health Extension Program

Ethiopia's Health Extension Program (HEP) was launched in 2003 in the four major agrarian regions of the country and later tailored and scaled up for pastoral and urban communities. The government developed it to be the main vehicle for achieving universal coverage of primary health care. The motivations for HEP included: low coverage of high-impact interventions; low access to health services, particularly by the rural poor, as well as an overall shortage of health workers; and weak institutional synergies to expand primary health care. HEP is now fully integrated into the broader health system and is an integral part of the Primary Health Care Unit structure. The program delivers 16 defined packages of preventive, promotive, and basic curative services. All its services are free and available to all.

Health extension workers (HEWs) are the key players in the program. They are all female, 10th grade high school graduates, and recruited from the community (with its help). They are trained for a year and then deployed back into the community to promote health and provide services at the village level. Much of their time is spent on home visits and outreach. Since HEP was launched, over 35,000 HEWs have been recruited, trained, and deployed to villages, and 15,000 health posts have been built and equipped, again with community participation and contributions.

Since its rollout, HEP has shown positive results in areas related to disease prevention, family health, hygiene, and environmental sanitation, but faces challenges. These include improving the quality of its services; enhancing skills and performance of the HEWs, particularly in maternal health; and sustaining the program with an appropriate career structure for the HEWs.

Source: Universal health coverage country summary report for Ethiopia, http://www.worldbank.org/en/topic/health/brief /uhc-japan.

and training requirements to ensure quality of care. Data and research in this area remain extremely patchy even in high-income countries, and deserve more attention from health policy makers and researchers.

Ensuring Equitable Distribution of Health Workers

All 11 countries are grappling with maldistribution of health workers, but those in Groups 1 and 2 especially so. Countries in Group 3 have, though, made large improvements in reducing geographic disparities.

Countries that have had relative success in reducing rural-urban disparities have done so through multiple strategies that address health workers' career aspirations via monetary and nonmonetary incentives, as well as improvements to working conditions and supportive supervision in health facilities (Araujo and Maeda 2013). These strategies include recruiting students from underserved areas and encouraging their enrollment through scholarships; setting quotas in schools; ensuring that curricula include rural service components; offering monetary and nonmonetary support for career development; and using governance policies to assign health workers to rural areas. Although the last approach can be susceptible to political influence and interest-group politics, mechanisms can reduce these influences, including a lottery system (as in Ethiopia and Turkey), or compulsory service through bonding. Countries in Group 3 have used a combination of these policies, and many of those in Group 2 are developing and pursuing policies with a similar, multipronged approach.

Another important strategic approach is to invest in primary care workers, both because investments in the hospital sector tend to skew the health workforce distribution toward urban areas and because investments in these health workers have additive benefits for health outcomes. All Group 3 countries have followed that strategy in expanding coverage and reducing regional disparities. Brazil made major investments in its Family Health Strategy (ESF) and Community Health Agents Program (PACS), which have contributed to achieving near-universal coverage over the last decade. Turkey too has narrowed geographic disparities, notably through its Family Medicine Program, which emphasizes primary care (box 6.2).

Another Group 3 country, Thailand, faced a 21-fold difference in physician density between Bangkok and the rural northeast regions several decades ago. Thus from 1975 it introduced financial incentives in the form of monthly hardship allowances for rural recruitment and rural retention with a focus on primary care services; since 1997 these allowances have been adjusted to

---

Box 6.2 Turkey's Strategy for Reducing Regional Disparities in the Health Workforce

Turkey's Family Medicine Program, which was rolled out nationwide in 2010, encourages doctors and other health workers to serve among rural populations. When family medicine physicians have registered patients in rural areas, midwives are assigned to them. In addition, periodic mobile outreach services are provided to those who live in rural areas.

The monthly base payment of family medicine physicians is adjusted for the socioeconomic level of their area of practice. Family medicine physicians working in underserved areas receive a "service credit" on a sliding scale, also linked to the socioeconomic development index of the district. In the least advantageous areas, the service credit can be as high as 40 percent of the maximum base payment. Since the introduction of the Family Medicine Program, disparities in the distribution of health personnel across the country have declined.

Enforcement of compulsory service for all public and private medical school graduates is another factor contributing to improving geographic distribution. Further, the Regulation on Appointment and Transfer ensures more balanced distribution of health care personnel across all Ministry of Health care facilities. Under this regulation, specialists, general practitioners, dentists, and pharmacists are appointed through a computer-based lottery, and other personnel are appointed by a central examination conducted in accordance with general provisions.

Source: Universal health coverage country summary report for Turkey, http://www.worldbank.org/en/topic/health/brief /uhc-japan.

---

reflect inflation and differentiated by hardship levels. By 2009 the difference in physician density had been reduced to five times (and that for nurses from 18 to 3 times).

Disparities in remuneration—distinctions between public and private sector salaries and benefits—are common in all countries in which mixed private and public health exists and are linked inextricably to the particular health system organization generally and labor market specifically in each country. This is important because remuneration of health workers is one of the key factors affecting recruitment (attractiveness of the profession), job satisfaction, and retention. It also can lead to dual practice—that is, health workers employed in government health facilities also working in the private sector, either in individual practice or other clinics or hospitals.

Dual practice is widespread in LMICs, and is emerging as a major issue in addressing health worker availability and distribution (Gruen 2002). Indonesia legalized dual practice as a way to promote the availability of health workers in the face of tight fiscal policies. This policy appears to have contributed to increasing the number and availability of private health care providers, but it may also be contributing to market segmentation, with the poor going to public facilities and the rich going to private providers (Anderson, Meliala, and Marzoeki, forthcoming). Turkey, on the other hand, has taken steps to ban dual practice while raising salaries for public sector health workers. Thus dual practice may help increase recruitment and retention of health workers who might otherwise migrate or move to other job markets, but unregulated dual practice could also exacerbate inequitable coverage. While there are widely different views on whether dual practice hinders or promotes access to health services, evidence on its impact on the health workforce remains limited (Araujo, Mahat, and Lemiere 2013).

Perceived low remuneration can also lead to movement of clinicians to non-health occupations within the country or to migration abroad (for health or nonhealth jobs). Other approaches include setting remuneration for workers at public facilities high enough to attract and retain competent graduates of health professional schools, particularly to provide care to underserved populations, as in rural or remote areas. However, any increase in health worker salaries is necessarily in the country context of competing needs and interests. Alternative, nonfinancial incentives such as continuing education and workplace conditions have been identified by clinicians as important, but only few data are available on their impact on retaining workers (Araujo and Maeda 2013).

Globalization of the health labor market has greatly increased mobility of health workers across national borders, requiring countries to consider this broader global health labor market when formulating their health workforce policies. Emigration of health workers is heavy for countries in Groups 1 and 2, but seems less of an issue for those in Groups 3 and 4 (figure 6.2). Since 2006, Ghana has pursued a strategy of investing in training, significantly increasing salaries, and incentive packages for health personnel working in rural and remote areas. The efforts appear to have contributed to an increase in the number of

Figure 6.2 Expatriation Rates of Doctors and Nurses, c. 2000

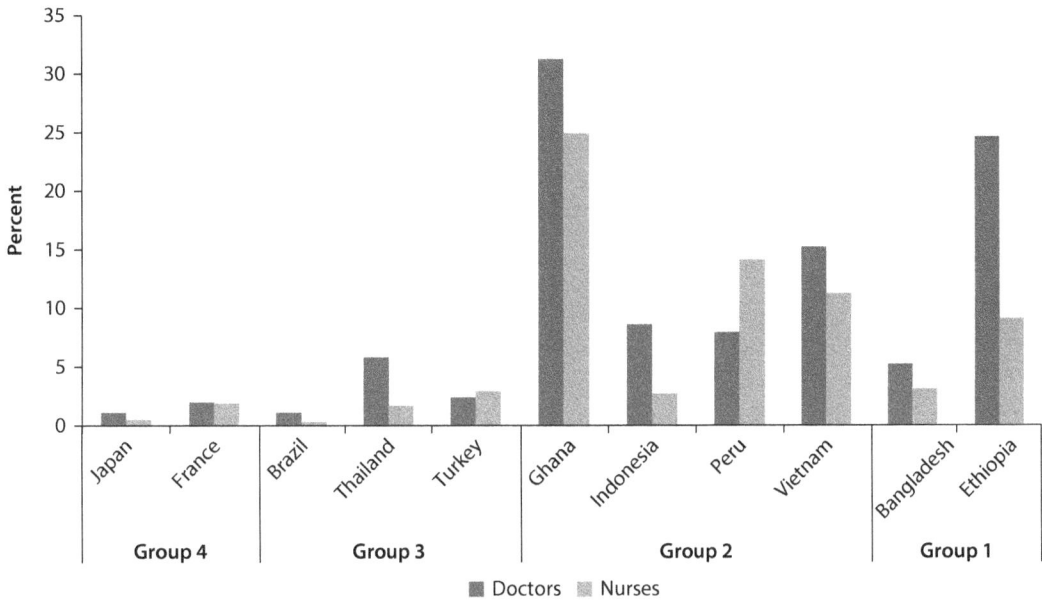

Source: OECD 2012.
Note: "Expatriation rate" refers to the percentage of the category of workers living outside their country at a given time. Data are for 2000.

students entering medical professionals and a decline in the number of physicians emigrating. When Thailand had to contend with a rapidly growing private sector and a strong pull from abroad, the government raised remuneration for public sector health workers (with a nonprivate practice incentive in 1995 and a long-term service allowance in 2005).

Improving Health Worker Performance

Policy makers need to understand health workforce performance and its determinants if they are to begin to address shortcomings and build on strengths. While comprehensive global evidence is lacking, partial evidence suggests that performance is far from optimal in most countries, irrespective of national income. Quantifying that performance would provide key data to guide education reform as well as inform changes in the system of incentives, human resources management, and broader labor market issues. Yet this is an area little studied in the health workforce literature, and there is a global lack of data and studies on measuring health worker performance, as well as a paucity of evidence on identifying what can be done to improve individual and team performance.

The regulatory systems for standards for accrediting health worker training schools, for the caliber and availability of faculty, for the examination and licensing/registering process, and for recertification (if any) are important in health workforce quality. Countries in Groups 1 and 2 face major constraints from education systems unable to produce enough graduates meeting minimum national quality standards. These countries are seeing a rapid increase in education institutions, which is creating new challenges in developing the human capacity to assure the quality of training content and of graduates. Without appropriate accreditation by a government or independent agency of public or private academic, degree-offering institutions, or schools that offer short-term training or certificate programs, governments risk compromising curriculum quality. Countries also need to invest in the continuing education of the existing cohort of health workers to ensure that their knowledge and skills stay abreast of medical advances, including setting requirements for continuing education and accreditation of the institutions through which it is offered.

Das, Hammer, and Leonard (2008) noted the complex nature of health worker performance in the context of multifaceted health systems, pointing to the importance of addressing the "three gaps": the knowledge needed by the health workers (need to know); the motivation needed for the health workers to use their knowledge effectively in a clinical setting (need to motivate); and the availability of basic supplies and infrastructure to enable health workers to provide services that meet the minimum standards of care. This requires effective management at the front line—from the highest levels of government throughout the system—and alignment and coordination of multiple policies and programs.

Nonmonetary incentives appear to be as important as monetary incentives, often relating to health workers' career development aspirations and working environment. Examples of nonmonetary incentives linked to job satisfaction, and so indirectly to quality of care, are: individualized mentoring using evidence-based clinical mentoring practices; periodic performance reviews with specific feedback and development plans; opportunities for continuing education (including the free time needed); career structures that offer the potential for promotion to posts with additional responsibilities and rewards; mechanisms for professional licensing of public and private sector workers; and verbal and other nonmonetary recognition of good performance.

Linking payments or other forms of incentives to health worker performance is becoming increasingly important in countries at all stages of UHC. Turkey has increased the overall number, productivity, and redistribution of health professionals through multifaceted interventions including contract-based employment, a mandatory service law, performance-based pay, and regulation of family medicine practice (Aran and Rokx, forthcoming). These policies have been largely successful at increasing the availability of health staff at public facilities, and redistributing human resources to regions with previously lower access. Overall, consultations per physician per year—a crude measure of productivity—increased from 2,272 in 2002 to 3,176 in 2006 and to 4,850 in 2011 (Ministry of Health, Turkey 2011). However these policies have also generated criticisms—especially among health professionals—that these gains have come at the cost of quality of care.

Thailand similarly has applied multiple approaches, including enhancing professional ethos among the government health workforce, offering financial incentives (overtime rates, hardship allowances, non-private-practice incentives, and long-service allowances) and nonfinancial incentives (social prestige and recognition, such as an annual prize for the best rural doctor or nurse), supporting career advancement, and permitting dual practice (where off-hours private practice is permitted). Even in a high-income country such as France, health workers' efficiency and quality of care have been a priority concern, especially with rising health care costs, tighter budget constraints, and the need to protect equity (box 6.3).

Box 6.3 France's Experience with Pay for Performance and Group Practice

Recent reforms in France have focused on improving the performance of health workers through multiple approaches to incentivize them and by reforming the governance structure to enhance accountability. The performance challenges were particularly high in the relatively unregulated primary care system, where most general practitioners (GPs) work in solo practices. Finding an effective way of funding group practices with an emphasis on prevention and care coordination in primary care has long been a policy objective, but despite several initiatives, their uptake has been very slow: fewer than 40 percent of generalists currently work in group practices, and the size of practices and their distribution vary widely by region.

In 2009, the government introduced a pilot scheme—Contracts for Improved Individual Practice, or CAPI (*Contrats d'amélioration des pratiques individuelles*)—which contracts primary care physicians on a performance-based payment system to encourage prevention and generic prescribing. CAPI was generalized to all GPs in 2011. It induced a change in French medical culture, demanding accountability from primary care providers for their results. But evaluation data show that while the results for prevention and for diabetes improved to some degree for all generalists, the difference between CAPI signatories and control cases was not significant.

In 2010, France introduced pilot projects on enhanced multidisciplinary group practice *Expérimentation de nouveaux modes de rémunération* (ENMR) to promote greater collaboration between physicians and paramedics, including task shifting across professional groups. Preliminary results suggest that the quality of care (prevention, coordination) in most domains is better, with slightly lower health care or pharmaceutical consumption in group practices than with solo-practice GPs. The analysis also suggests that in areas where pilots were installed, the density of GPs grew faster than in control areas.

These contrasting experiences suggest that payment reforms alone may be insufficient to elicit better performance from health workers, especially when the care delivery model (such as solo practice) does not provide a basis for the multidisciplinary teams required to manage preventive care and coordination across different levels of care.

Source: Barroy et al., forthcoming.

Universal Health Coverage for Inclusive and Sustainable Development
http://dx.doi.org/10.1596/978-1-4648-0297-3

References

Anderson, I., A. Meliala, and P. Marzoeki. Forthcoming. "The Production, Distribution, and Performance of Physicians, Nurses, and Midwives in Indonesia." World Bank, Washington, DC.

Aran, M., and C. Rokx. Forthcoming. "Turkey on the Way of Universal Health Coverage through the Health Transformation Program (2003–2013)." World Bank, Washington, DC.

Araujo, E., and A. Maeda. 2013. "How to Recruit and Retain Health Workers in Rural and Remote Areas in Developing Countries: A Guidance Note." HNP Discussion Paper, World Bank, Washington, DC.

Araujo, E., A. Mahat, and C. Lemiere. 2013. "Guidance Note on Dual Practice in Healthcare." HNP Discussion Paper, World Bank, Washington, DC.

Barroy, H., Z. Or, A. Kumar, and D. Bernstein. Forthcoming. "Sustaining Universal Health Coverage in France: A Perpetual Challenge." World Bank, Washington, DC.

Das, J., J. Hammer, and K. L. Leonard. 2008. "The Quality of Medical Advice in Low Income Countries." *Journal of Economic Perspectives* 22 (2).

GHWA and WHO (Global Health Workforce Alliance and World Health Organization). 2013. *A Universal Truth: No Health without a Workforce.* Geneva: WHO.

Gruen, R. A. 2002. "Dual Job Holding Practitioners in Bangladesh: An Exploration." *Social Sciences in Medicine* 54 (2): 267–79.

Ikegami, N., ed. Forthcoming. *Universal Health Coverage for Inclusive and Sustainable Development: Lessons from Japan.* Washington, DC: World Bank.

McPake, B., A. Maeda, E. C. Araujo, C. Lemiere, A. Al-Maghreby, and G. Cometto. 2013. "Why Do Health Labor Market Forces Matter?" *Bulletin of the World Health Organization* 91: 841–46. doi: http://dx.doi.org/10.2471/BLT.13.118794.

Ministry of Health, Turkey. 2011. *Turkey Health Transformation Program Evaluation Report 2003–2010.* Ankara.

OECD (Organisation for Economic Co-operation and Development). 2012. *Connecting with Emigrants—A Global Profile of Diasporas* (accessed September 1, 2013). http://www.oecd-ilibrary.org/social-issues-migration-health/connecting-with-emigrants/expatriation-rates-for-nurses-and-doctors-circa-2000-table_9789264177949-table181-en.

WDI (World Development Indicators). 2013. http://data.worldbank.org/data-catalog/world-development-indicators.

WHO (World Health Organization). 2006. *The World Health Report 2006—Working Together for Health.* Geneva.

———. 2013. Global Health Observatory Data Repository (accessed June 1, 2013). http://apps.who.int/gho/data/view.main.

CHAPTER 7

Key Issues and Next Steps

Cross-Cutting Issues

The country studies suggest that implementation of universal health coverage (UHC) strategies involves interacting with multiple interest groups that influence decisions on the design and implementation of programs, including key decisions on budget allocation and investments in the health workforce. Progress toward UHC involves constant adjustments to find a balance between making strategic compromises and implementing a sustainable path to equitable health coverage. This calls for *adaptive leadership*—one that considers the perspectives of the multiple interest groups in designing and planning UHC strategy—as an essential element for successfully adopting and sustaining these efforts.

Policies that reflect the perspectives of different interest groups may lead to a technically suboptimal but politically feasible solution. Political compromises may weaken the impact of some policies on UHC objectives or exacerbate potential unintended consequences. For these reasons, it will be critical to have an effective system for monitoring and evaluating progress toward UHC to identify these trends, inform communities, and enable policy makers to take the necessary corrective measures.

Defining the benefits package and the depth and scope of services covered under UHC is one of the most challenging issues that policy makers face in designing and executing UHC strategy. The approach has to go beyond defining services covered, to include levels of subsidization and copayments, choice of health care providers, and conditions for reimbursement. These benefits need to be translated into services on the ground, with appropriately skilled workers and financing systems as well as sufficient medicines, technology, and infrastructure.

It is important to lead with a strong commitment to primary health care and public health programs in tandem with careful cost management. The effective rollout of universal coverage in Group 3 countries has been enabled by a strong tradition of local primary care. Brazil's Family Health Strategy gave high priority to providing quality primary care coverage to families where access had been lacking. This has helped avoid situations that contribute to cost escalation, for example when patients sidestep clinics that provide primary care and go directly to secondary and tertiary hospitals designed to treat more complex or severe cases, where care is more costly. Thus focusing the UHC strategy on primary health care and community-based public health programs accomplishes multiple objectives: health service access and financial protection are improved at the initial point of contact with beneficiaries; resources are directed to more cost-effective services including public health risk mitigation and health promotion; and overall costs in the system can be more easily managed.

Provider payment policies and systems are crucial in directing resources and creating incentives for quality, equity, and efficiency, and countries are increasingly moving away from supply-side budgeting (financing of inputs) toward demand-based payments and output-based payments that link expenditures not to inputs but to results (outputs and outcomes). These payment systems require parallel investments in institutional and technical capacity to conduct independent audits and service reviews, and are necessary to mitigate supplier-induced demand (use of unnecessary procedures) and to promote safety and adherence to quality standards in health care.

Reforms to payment systems also require concurrent reforms in governance of the health care delivery system to address some of the structural constraints, such as rigid civil service structures and public finance systems, which can constrain providers from responding to the incentives created by the reformed payment systems. Examples include governance reforms in government-run hospitals (as in France and Japan) and contracting-out of services when internal reforms are hard to achieve (such as primary health care contracting in Brazil).

The following sections review some cross-cutting issues by country groups.

Group 1 Countries

These two countries—Bangladesh and Ethiopia—face multiple challenges of low gross domestic product (GDP) per capita and low revenue mobilization as a share of GDP, which tends to lead to high out-of-pocket spending, dependence of government facilities on user fees and/or unofficial payments, and limitations in technical capacity and accountability mechanisms. They are struggling with expanding very basic health prevention and promotion services, and face major constraints of acute health workforce shortages and restricted financial resources.

Still, their experience points to the importance of using a combination of supply-side interventions, strengthened community outreach and accountability, innovative financing (including performance payments), and other mechanisms to expand access to affordable primary health care services and public health programs.

Their initial challenge is to find innovative approaches to UHC, including expanding the health care workforce quickly at relatively low cost and directed to reaching underserved areas, while striving to ensure quality and effectiveness of care. Equally, these countries are moving toward introducing demand-side interventions through the introduction of third-party payers, which requires investments in new technical and institutional capacity with potential increases in administrative costs and complexities. Ethiopia's effort to scale up training and deployment of health extension workers and to concentrate attention on primary care services is exemplary from this perspective. The decisions initiated at this early stage of UHC can have long-term repercussions on the development of the health system.

It may be instructive for Bangladesh and Ethiopia to examine the experiences of Group 2 countries tackling the problems created by their earlier decisions that have led to highly fragmented health systems, as both are considering introducing social health insurance as the financing vehicle for expanding coverage, which could result in preferential coverage for formal sector workers and exclusion of households in the informal sector.

Group 2 Countries

These four countries—Ghana, Indonesia, Peru, and Vietnam—have made large strides toward expanding coverage and building institutional capacities, but they often end up with multiple health programs with different benefits and delivery systems. They face uncovered population groups, mostly in the informal sector, which existing programs find hard to reach. These countries are taking steps to integrate or harmonize their different systems, and are looking for approaches to reach the remaining uncovered groups. Learning from the experiences of Group 3 and 4 countries may be helpful, notably in how those two groups extended coverage to the informal sector and other hard-to-reach population groups, and how they managed to integrate or harmonize multiple programs. Ghana has already taken steps to integrate through its National Health Insurance Scheme (NHIS); similarly, Indonesia and Peru are preparing to integrate their health funds in one national health insurance system. Vietnam is reviewing its fragmented payment system and considering options to take a more coordinated approach to aligning payment incentives at all levels of the health system.

Group 3 Countries

Brazil, Thailand, and Turkey have achieved UHC on population coverage. They have attained significant coverage expansion through a strong emphasis on primary health care, redistribution of resources to reduce inequities in coverage, and efforts to recruit and retain health workers in underserved communities. These countries are now facing new challenges in managing expenditures to meet the growing demand from the population for more comprehensive coverage and higher quality care. They face accelerating cost pressures, rising demand for quality services from a growing middle class, and the consequences of aging populations with a higher burden of chronic diseases. Another key issue is regulating the role of the private sector in UHC, both as payer (private insurance) and provider. Brazil has allowed the private insurance market to expand rapidly, while the public sector struggles to provide quality services, as reflected in continuing high out-of-pocket spending by Brazilian households. The emergence of a two-tier system could also undermine equitable coverage. Thailand and Turkey have

Universal Health Coverage for Inclusive and Sustainable Development
http://dx.doi.org/10.1596/978-1-4648-0297-3

restricted the role of private insurance by ensuring substantial funding through public resources to cover health care, but this, in turn, is putting mounting pressure on their government budgets.

Group 4 Countries

This group's two countries—France and Japan—have a long history with UHC and well-established institutions, but rapid advances in technology combined with aging populations and ever-tightening budget resources are putting new pressures on their systems. These pressures are forcing them to seek ways to improve the performance of the health system, manage costs, and maintain equitable UHC. France is struggling with fiscal constraints and cost-containment issues, while Japan is facing a small but growing number of people who are not covered, as well as growing disparities in contribution rates among households. Both are considering (and have undertaken some) reform measures. Their experiences point to the need for continuous adjustments to maintain UHC in the face of changing economic and demographic structures.

Next Steps

UHC offers great opportunities for reducing poverty and securing the health care needs of a country's lower-income groups. To exploit this potential, each country needs to develop an adaptive health system with solid institutional foundations and governance, leaders with the vision to take advantage of these opportunities and the will to support them, and an engaged civil society that demands accountability and transparency as a check against institutional weakness and interest-group politics. Technocratic solutions need to be matched by careful strategic planning that takes account of these and other political economy issues.

The World Bank Group, with support from the government of Japan and other partner governments and agencies, is committed to helping countries make informed decisions and investments in achieving their UHC goals. A number of initiatives and actions are proposed to take this agenda forward. The World Health Organization (WHO) and the World Bank Group are collaborating closely to develop a framework for measuring progress toward UHC (WHO and World Bank 2013). Training and capacity-building programs for policy makers and policy analysts will be provided through courses such as the World Bank Institute's Flagship Course on UHC. There will be support for joint learning platforms and practices to help countries articulate their demand for technical assistance and information, and encourage systematic exchange of knowledge and experiences among countries.

The ultimate objective of these programs will be to assist countries to set their own priorities and assess progress toward UHC, and to offer a knowledge platform that promotes effective learning across countries. The experiences of countries examined as part of the Japan–World Bank Partnership Program for UHC make clear that attaining UHC is a complex process, fraught with challenges, many possible paths, and multiple possible pitfalls—but that it is feasible.

There is no single solution, but countries can be better prepared, and therefore have a better chance of succeeding, if they start with political commitment and a clear understanding of the political economy challenges, enabling them to undertake coverage-enhancing reform that remains sustainable over the long run.

Reference

WHO and World Bank. 2013. "Monitoring Progress towards Universal Health Coverage at Country and Global Levels: A Framework." A discussion paper. http://www .who.int/healthinfo/country_monitoring_evaluation/UHC_WBG_DiscussionPaper _Dec2013.pdf.

Environmental Benefits Statement

The World Bank Group is committed to reducing its environmental footprint. In support of this commitment, the Publishing and Knowledge Division leverages electronic publishing options and print-on-demand technology, which is located in regional hubs worldwide. Together, these initiatives enable print runs to be lowered and shipping distances decreased, resulting in reduced paper consumption, chemical use, greenhouse gas emissions, and waste.

The Publishing and Knowledge Division follows the recommended standards for paper use set by the Green Press Initiative. Whenever possible, books are printed on 50 percent to 100 percent postconsumer recycled paper, and at least 50 percent of the fiber in our book paper is either unbleached or bleached using Totally Chlorine Free (TCF), Processed Chlorine Free (PCF), or Enhanced Elemental Chlorine Free (EECF) processes.

More information about the Bank's environmental philosophy can be found at http://crinfo.worldbank.org/wbcrinfo/node/4.

green
press
INITIATIVE